The Lemurian Science of Peace

Entering the Higher Reality of Mastery

Almine

Published by Spiritual Journeys LLC

First Edition December 2013

Copyright 2013

MAB 998 Megatrust
By Almine
Spiritual Journeys LLC
P.O. Box 300
Newport, Oregon 97365

US toll-free phone: 1-877-552-5646

www.spiritualjourneys.com

All rights reserved. No part of this publication may be reproduced without written permission of the publishers.

Cover art - Charles Frizzell

Manufactured in the United States of America

ISBN 978-1-936926-89-3 Softcover
ISBN 978-1-936926-90-9 Adobe Reader

Table of Contents

Introduction v

Book I – The Science of Peace
Achieving Peace Through Balancing the Sub-personalities 3
    The Sub-personalities 4
Overcoming the Cause of Pain – Separate Polarities 9
    The Overcoming of Conflict 10
    The Birth of Death 12
Stepping off the Treadmill – The Origin of Stress 15
    The Busy Treadmill 16
The Deeper Mysteries of Existence Part I 23
Overcoming the Hold of the Past – Stepping into Freedom 47
    The Prison Bars of Man 48
    The Mystical Relationships of the Cosmos 51
    The Relationship Between Cosmoses 54
    Relationship Types that Ensnare 56
    The Four Stages of Conflict Resolution 62
The Deeper Mysteries of Existence Part II 67
Learning to Live with Diversity 83
    Understanding the Differences 88

Book II – Freedom from the Treadmill
Introduction 101
The History of the Cycles 105
    Introduction to the History of the Cycles 106
The Eighteen Cycles of Existence 109
Closing of the History of the Cycles 250

Book III – Living from the Dodecahedral Fields and Beyond

The Ancient Lemurian Records of Life and Death 255
- Part I   *Nana Nech Bavi Ursata* – Naught is as it Seems 256
- Part II   *Karus Haresta Pravechbi Unes* – The Root of the Antagonism of the Poles 258
- Part III   *Naruk Sachve Ereshti* – The Song of the Five Elements 261
- Part IV   *Nesetuk Maneshve* – The Lost Song 263
- Part V   *Kashu Anach Savati* – The Unlived Possibilities 265
- Part VI   *Spehesbave Nenuk Harasat* – The Power of Language 267
  - The Body of Magical Incantations from the Mother of All Creation 279
- Part VII   *Parsu Nenechva Harstusat* – The Origins of Guilt ... 296
- Part VIII   *Kalesh Archba Rerukva-ba* – Understanding What Opposites Are 298
- Part IX   *Arech Pa Haretu Ninasvi* – Allowing Life to Sing ... 300
  - The Tuft of Flowers by Robert Frost 302
- Part X   *Nechbar Misitrechve* – Seeing the Unseen 304
- Part XI   *Bri-u-esh Aranach Uvesbi* – Expectations of Glad Adventure 306
- Part XII   *Persklahit Nenechvi Aruvas* – The Evolutionary Leap 308
- Part XIII   *Nuch-tarava Mishtu Aravas* – The Deceit of Reality Unravels 310

Closing 312

Introduction

The depth and width of the information that has been translated from the Lemurian tablets and scrolls to produce the Science of Peace is breathtaking in its scope.

Each specific set of records I have translated over the years has had its own dominant trait and a characteristic method of delivery. (See www.interdimensionalphotos.com for interdimensional photos of some of these records.) Some poured in at such a rate that I could hardly write fast enough. Some came as glyphs, visible a few feet in front of my face. Others were downloading the glyphs at night and repeating the language in audio form during the day.

The Science of Peace has had the specific quality of being very concise and articulate. They were written in one of the primary cosmic languages, not Lemurian. They are engraved in pale pinkish, highly polished stone tablets with a set of two scrolls giving the information of the last part of the book.

The delivery of the information was accompanied by a steady pressure in my chest, indicating that the translation was time-sensitive; I was on a schedule. The advent of this profound and sacred material is accompanied by a destiny: to bring peace on Earth.

BOOK I

The Science of Peace

Achieving Peace through Balancing the Sub-personalities

The destiny of humanity is to bring peace to the great diversity of life forms on Earth. The establishing of a safe and happy global home for all creatures begins by creating peace within the Inner Family: the sub-personalities of man.

The Sub-personalities

The most successful components of tribalism have been their stability and predictability. But this has come at a cost – lack of growth and danger of stagnation. The stable patterns of the relationships within the tribe depend on everyone playing their role. The tribe is therefore based on dependency.

Dependency is the most elemental form of social development: the dependence of the chick on the boundaries of the egg – both the chick and the egg depending for their existence on one another. The mother and infant are a closely bonded tribe, neither straying too far from one another. The contentment within this stage is deep, and so is the scarring to the psyche if premature disruption occurs.

Eventually life pressures the tribe to evolve further, but because of the contentment, tribal members resist. Forced and painful proddings are eventually needed to birth life to the next level.

Our sub-personalities are our inner tribe: the Inner Child, Inner Elder or Sage, the Inner Nurturer and the Inner Warrior. Tribal social structures have mimicked these inner relationships.

The center of the tribe consists of the children. Around them, like a protective circle, are the Elders. They guide and listen to the Children and report to the Nurturers if something is wrong. Around them are the Nurturers who care for the Elders and the Children. The outer ring consists of the Warriors who protect the whole tribe from outer and inner hostile or subversively hostile influences.

The man in the street finds his own tribe: the drinking buddies at the pub, the clubs and cause-driven associations, family units or social groups. The variety is great in tribes that form, but all of them have uniformity of some kind in common.

When diversity enters the tribe, it is threatened and must either repel the new element or embrace diversity within uniformity. This created a conflict between individuality and tribal control and becomes co-dependence. The two-year old enters this stage in which the parents attempt to control his behavior and he or she tries to thwart their control.

The spiritual seeker who evolves into this stage, questions established religions' teachings and authority. The stage beyond this, complete independence, can create a shunning of all spirituality and a materialistic and egocentric approach to life. It is for this reason that teenagers seem to consider no one but themselves.

The more conscious person evolves into interdependency – unity within diversity. During this stage there is cooperation with others on mutually agreed projects (such as raising children together) while individuality is supported and encouraged.

The inner family must also evolve through these stages for an integrated, dynamically balanced human being. One of the biggest pitfalls in interacting with others is the possible occurrence of the Dr. Jekyll and Mr. Hyde syndrome: The unintegrated sub-personalities can cause a split in the personality and the pleasant person can change into an irrational and hostile one.

How to Balance the Sub-personalities

Firstly, get to know the sub-personality that is expressing and find the ones that are not. If we have been used to others telling us what is holy or channelling our guidance, our inner sage may be dormant. Resist the temptation of allowing others to tell you how to live and allow time for the still communion with the all-knowing depths of your being.

If programmed beliefs have told you that a 'holy' life is to serve others at the expense of yourself, your nurturer needs to be resurrected. Begin with small acts of self-nurturing or have your warrior establish, in small ways at first, your healthy boundaries.

Secondly, gauge the degree of evolution you have achieved by the way your sub-personalities interact.

1. **Dependency:** This stage produces defense mechanisms to shield the Inner Child. It may for instance pacify a belligerent person in order not to get 'hurt'. It will try and fit in with the tribe.

2. **Co-dependency:** This stage is marked by control. Most relationships are co-dependent – the reason that most end badly. Co-dependent behavior is based on a triangle. Leg one consists of "I give all that I can". Leg two says, "Because I give so much, I get to control you". Leg three is outraged and angry when the person they are trying to control will not let them. The nurturer may tell the child when it may or may not express. The sage may tell the warrior it is not 'spiritual' to become angry.

3. **Independency:** The value of the diverse sub-personalities is recognized. Each gets its own time to express. The individual expression of sub-personalities, like anything that cannot freely express, is usually more exaggerated during this stage.

4. **Interdependence:** Life during this stage unfolds with more grace and less conflict. This is because the inner battles for individual control ceases within the sub-personalities. The childlike charm can help the inner warrior state a boundary that must not be crossed with ease. All sub-personalities express with ease and in a mutually beneficial way.

Each one of us knows that life can be so much easier; our deepest truths whisper that conflict as a tool of growth, can be transcended. The answer lies in the sub-personalities – the inner family of man. Only there can peace on Earth begin.

Expressing the Sub-personalities

- To get to know them, express them individually, allotting time for each.
- The second step is to allow them to express in all areas of life – let the nurturer into your workplace by having little comforts in your environment: protein bars in your drawer, a soft throw blanket to cover your legs tucked under your desk. Take the sage with you on your commute to work by listening to inspiring music or words, for example.
- Eventually, through practiced expression, allow them to express all the time. The more they express, the more graceful they become. When they are not fully expressing, they become jagged.

Overcoming the Cause of Pain

Separate Polarities

When two poles exist, one thrives at the expense of the other. While living in polarity, life is subject to the law of compensation – the one gains at the expense of the other. This causes pain and guilt.

The Overcoming of Conflict

The law of compensation decrees that for every gain there is a loss. This places guilt on those who gain and pain for those who sustain the loss. Yet a loss cannot really ever occur, it is just that resources are passed around, the way the ball is passed around during a tennis match.

The answer to healing this tug of war between the pro-active and the receptive poles has many components.

Understanding the Masculine and Feminine

The pro-active, masculine role and the receptive, feminine role can be seen from three levels of perception:

The Lowest Perspective

The lowest level sees some creations as feminine, some as masculine. This creates a reality with great conflict as they battle for supremacy, or one abdicates its role in favor of the other. The second scenario provokes catastrophe to break up the resulting stagnation.

The Middle Perspective

Androgyny, or genderlessness, takes place when judgement that favors one pole over another ceases. At that time both poles express equally in dynamic balance. This means there is but a slight variance of emphases as one pole or another expresses. There is much less opposition and hardship in such a reality.

Within polarity we are cut off from the limitless resources of the indivisible Source. Resources are generated by the back and forth movement between the poles. Thus, where there is little movement between poles, resources decline and financial depressions could result.

The Highest Perspective

The poles become one in this stage. There is no tension between the poles. It is the gaps between breaths – the null point of existence in which there is no tomorrow or yesterday. There is just life unfolding now. Opposites and oneness are expressing simultaneously.

The moment is the place of self-sufficiency, where all dependence of any kind ceases. The moment is the fulcrum point of existence, where past and future meet, and life and death embrace. It contains all and creates all by dividing itself in a never-ending sequence, reflecting it outwards as our environment.

The moment is the one from which the many came; yet it does not exist. Any point has as itself a center point, which in turn has a center point, and so on into infinity.

Anything that has an opposite does not really exist, thus neither does the one nor the many.

The Birth of Death

From the *Saradesi Records of Life and Death*

Long have we fought duality's bain
Long have we sought to eliminate pain
By ridding ourself of separation and duality,
And linear time caused by polarity

From this desire transformation formed
From transformation death was born
Its role to eliminate the obsolete
Was caused by our inability to see

We saw the separation and thought it was wrong
We thought that in oneness we belong
Whenever opposites exist, real they cannot be
Separation is imagined by the way we see

Oneness and separation are each other's opposite
They can therefore in reality not exist
Let our eyes be healed from polarity
That oneness and separation both can be seen

There's space and spacelessness at the same time
To see this, eliminate mind
For it desires to know and catagorize
Separating oneness seen with our eyes

Experience life through the eyes of a child
Resist the temptation to categorize
Nought can be known or defined
It's just a lie conceived of by mind

All that exists can be imagined as separated
All has existed forever; hasn't been created
Yet only parts of what is, are expressing on stage
Off-stage all other players wait

Let it be known that what we resist
Will beyond its time continue to persist
The stage of life crowded became
Instead of in the wings, all players are on stage

Unbearable it feels, the pressure of life has become
Crowded and confusing and discordant to some
Reflected in bodies that become obese
Let the untimely presences now cease

Both poles as valid existing together
Means all that is, has been forever
When one is emphasized within the whole
The other still exists in a more dormant role

The proactive and dormant play out at one time
The past and the present are not in a line
They exist all at once; together they flow
Changelessly changing as life unfolds

Stepping off the Treadmill
The Origin of Stress

A life of grace and peace unfolds through inspiration rather than opposition. All life changes when we find our source of inspiration.

Almine

The Busy Treadmill

The imbalance of doingness and hyperactivity versus beingness and repose has several causes. One of the primary ones however, yet again finds its origin in the sub-personalities.

The model of the sub-personalities replicates the smallest building blocks of life, the sub-atomic particles. They in turn are microcosmic representations of the macrocosm: We live inside a massive tube torus; a doughnut shape that folds in and out upon itself and spins.

Native Americans call these in and out pulsations, the red road (like the blood that flows away from the heart) and the blue road (the venous system back to the heart). It is called the In-breath and Out-breath of God by the Hindu traditions.

Because we are all in different realities (like different slices of bread that altogether make up the loaf), we may choose to step out of this turning (and spinning) tube torus. The person whose reality participates in the spinning is in linear time – the cause of stress, aging and disease. The centrifugal force of the treadmill leaks resources much the same way that a spin-dryer removes moisture from the laundry.

The in and out movement, coupled with the boundaries formed by belief systems and worldviews, dictates a life that is cyclical and limited in the experiences that can be enjoyed. These limitations form the mortal boundaries that imprison most of humanity.

The cycles formed by this limited life are found in many forms, with life and death incarnations being the largest, and sleeping and awakening as the smallest. Mystics teach that challenges and victories come in 7, 13 and 20 year cycles.

But there is however another significant factor that urges us to step off the treadmill. The cosmos, or the life of an individual, spins around the center like a spinning top or a gyroscope. In your life it is your embodiment – you.

If we live in polarity, this motion also provides the energy and power needed to sustain life, since polarity cuts us off from the inexhaustible supply of resources from Source. To keep us energized, life keeps the energy producing tube toral spinning by exerting pressure on the center – you. This constitutes the reason our lives have been riddled with opposition.

The more steeped we are in belief systems, and hence the more programmed our behavior is, the more life pressures us to change through providing opposition. Belief systems thicken the walls of our cocoon and cut us off from the supply of resources from Source even more, thus making it necessary for life to spin even faster. The increased motion is accomplished by increased pressure on the center point.

For eons of existence a missing factor in the duty-driven lives of humanity has been the lack of authentic expression. This key component to a well-balanced life has been stifled by survival-orientated worldviews. The result is the suppression of certain sub-personalities as well as an imbalance in their polarities. Imbalance in these crucial components of the psyche is like a bump to the side of the spinning top that causes a wobble in the rotation. The top spins erratically and slows down. Now more pressure is needed to keep its movement going. It is for this reason that a balanced expression of the sub-personalities is vital to establishing a life of grace and peace that unfolds through inspiration rather than opposition.

One may well ask why we are balancing sub-personalities when they are themselves part of polarity, having masculine and feminine components. Nothing can transcend its present state if that state is one of imbalance. The reason for this is that life demands that our present state be fully actualized and have yielded its full potential before it transcends into a higher form of expression.

The I Ching, Tzolk'in or Kabbalah have mapped out the four more masculine, electric components by mapping out the developmental stages of life's[1] evolution. This mirrors the developmental stages of the psyche – the sub-personalities.

But because they have been unaware of the feminine, magnetic horizontal axis, these traditional models have only depicted the Inner Child, Inner Sage, Inner Nurturer and Inner Warrior. This ignores the sub-personalities that correspond to the horizontal axis.

The Sub-personalities of the Horizontal Axis

The sub-personalities of the cosmos are the directions. Indigenous people throughout the ages have acknowledged the 7 directions. The races have represented the 7 sub-personalities of the cosmos. The more physical races of the four directions represented the child, sage, nurturer and warrior. The tribes of man have done the same. The additional 3 directions of above, below and within of the horizontal, feminine axis have been represented by the unseen, more subtle races.

The sub-personalities of the additional three directions are the Inner Scout (above), Wild Woman (below) and the Inner Babe (the two year old boy representing within).

This has left the feminine within all of us with only three sub-personalities versus the four of the masculine axis. The law of polarity is also the law of compensation. It seeks equity. This is the contributing cause of the expansion and contraction movements of the tube torus. It is forever trying to compensate the inequity found between the masculine and feminine – like a dog chasing its tail, or a hamster on a treadmill.

In a master's reality, this inequity is finally solved: The highly conscious being has 8 sub-personalities and lives in a much different reality. He or she is able to stop linear time to a large extent. Besides the

---

1 See *Journey to the Heart of God*.

additional sub-personality, there is also a change in their polarity: their proactive and receptive qualities.

The additional sub-personality is Wise Woman – she who embodies the goddess archetypes. Wise Woman's 13 goddess archetypes[2] bring sacredness and reverence to life. Honored by tribes in Africa, North and South America and other traditions, the 13 facets bring fullness and texture to everyday life.

The Little Boy (the Inner Babe) is the adventurer, exploring the possibilities of life. He sees all things with the new eyes of wonderment. Without him life dwindles and ruts trap our awareness.

The Scout examines the broad consequences of actions, which is why he has also been called the High Mind or the Voice of Conscience. He is the innovator and the explorer of fulfilling new directions. His presence adds vigor to life and finds ways to walk a path that makes our hopes and desires possible.

Wild Woman is boundlessness in expression; the root of all magic and instinctual knowing. She holds in her heart the primordial beginnings of life. Her interpretative dance tells the secrets of existence and her breath breathes fertility into our journey.

The indescribable joy of a contented Inner Family in expression awaits all who are ready to leave the treadmill's adversity behind. It does not end duality but balances it – the next step to transcending to a life of no opposites.

---

2 See *A Life of Miracles*.

The Sub-personalities of Lower Consciousness

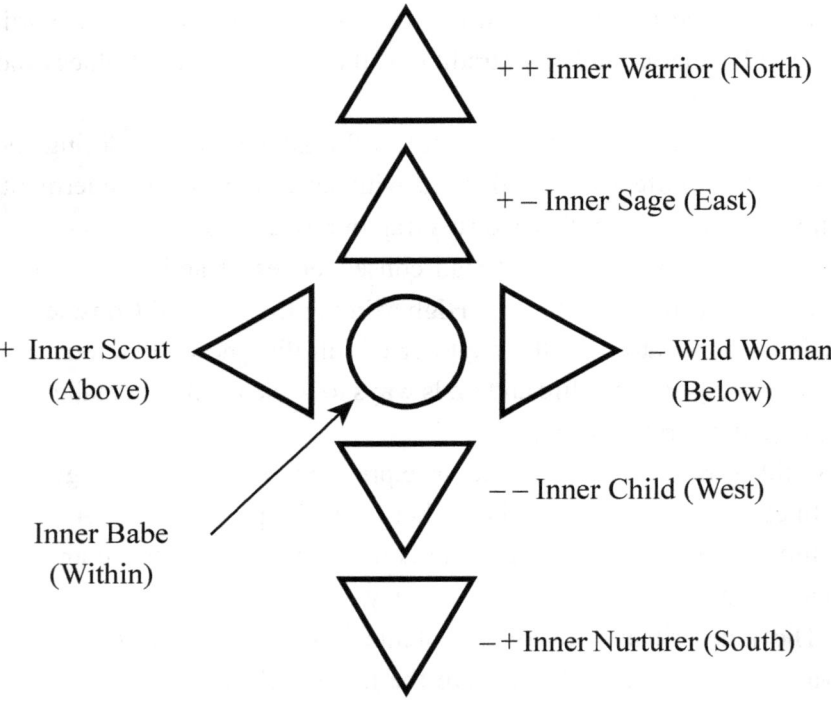

Note how the horizontal feminine axis is shorter.

Figure 1

The Sub-personalities of Higher Consciousness

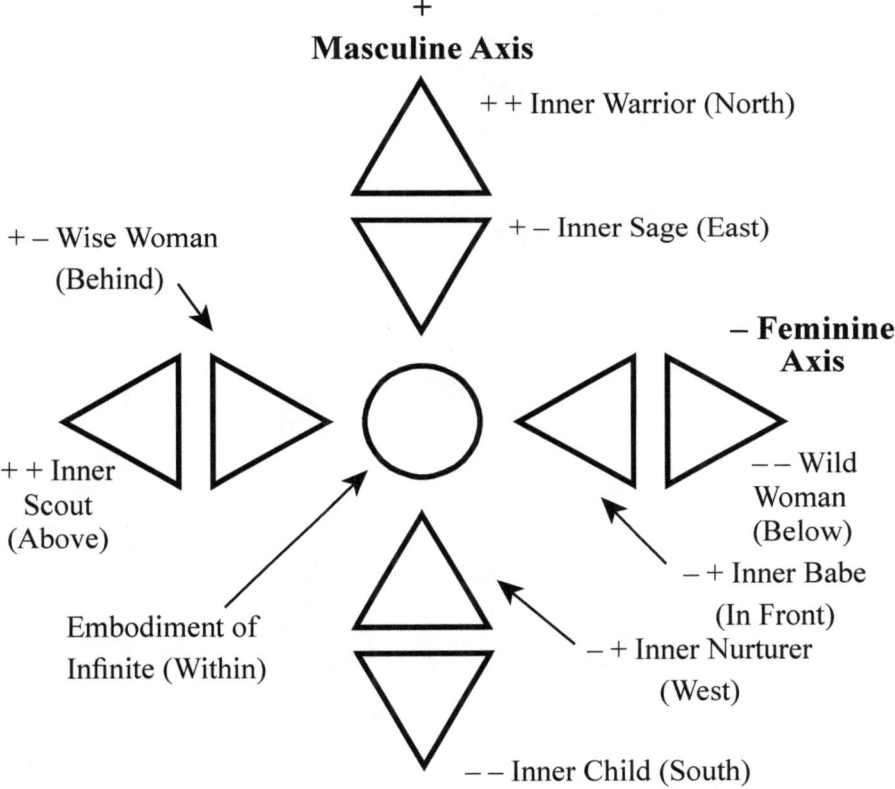

Although these relationships are depicted as flat, they are in fact rounded to make a tube torus. All pointed parts of the triangles are towards the middle circle – the central hole of the tube torus – when the axes bend over.

Figure 2

The Deeper Mysteries of Existence

Part I

The Records of Ananu

The Lemurian Tablets of Ananu speak of the eight dominant tones of Creation's directions:

1. The Inner Babe – Unselfconscious Spontaneity

2. The Wise Woman – Valuing all Experiences

3. The Wild Woman – Boundless Being

4. The Scout – Self-surrender

5. The Inner Child – Jubilance in Expression

6. The Inner Sage – Lightness of Being

7. The Inner Nurturer – Identityless Journey

8. The Inner Warrior – Agendaless Existence

9. The Embodiment of the Infinite – Consolidated Purpose

Stories of our lives can become identities if we allow them to define us. They are a role we briefly play on the stage of life, and as life moves to the next act, they disappear. Do not value them as relevant to who you are in the moment, but neither should they be discarded if they are a source of inspiration and a means of connecting with others.

In the records of Ananu, the masculine axis
of existence is called:

Enach varavi vruhespa
The Journey of Becoming

Book I – The Science of Peace

The feminine horizontal axis is called:

Pisiheresba kenevich manunet pavi
The Arrival at Endless Destinations

The inclination for the vertical axis is to become hyperactive and the horizontal one to stagnate.

The directions each have a specific evolutionary stage of life and consist of vast rivers of quantum, subatomic particles. These rivers are called the great bands of compassion. All stages of growth and evolution in life follow the precession of these qualities of the directions and consist of their building blocks.

Almine's Note: The four stages of dependency, co-dependency, independence and inter-dependence are well-known to most, but the additional 3 stages are not:

1. **Autonomy:** (diversity within unity) Whereas the frequency band of unity within diversity relies on a common vision to sustain the relationship, autonomy is based on being of one heart with diverse ideas and visions. Autonomy takes complete responsibility for the mirrors in the environment. Any external aspect is changed by changing the self.

2. **Divine Sovereignty:** (unity of heart and mind) This relationship pulses between two beings in a way that provides a continuous

energy source for both. When one is projecting through the heart, the other is receiving through the heart and projecting through the mind. The resulting energy enhances the consciousness of both.

3. **Self-sustaining Oneness:** (immovable oneness) The melding of minds and hearts into oneness is beyond unity. Unity, as described in Divine Sovereignty, presupposes an interaction that alternates, like a pulsation between receptivity and proactivity. Oneness forms a unified field where the language of love and light communicates not linearly, but as an immediate telepathic/empathic knowingness.

Where the Bands of Compassion Come From

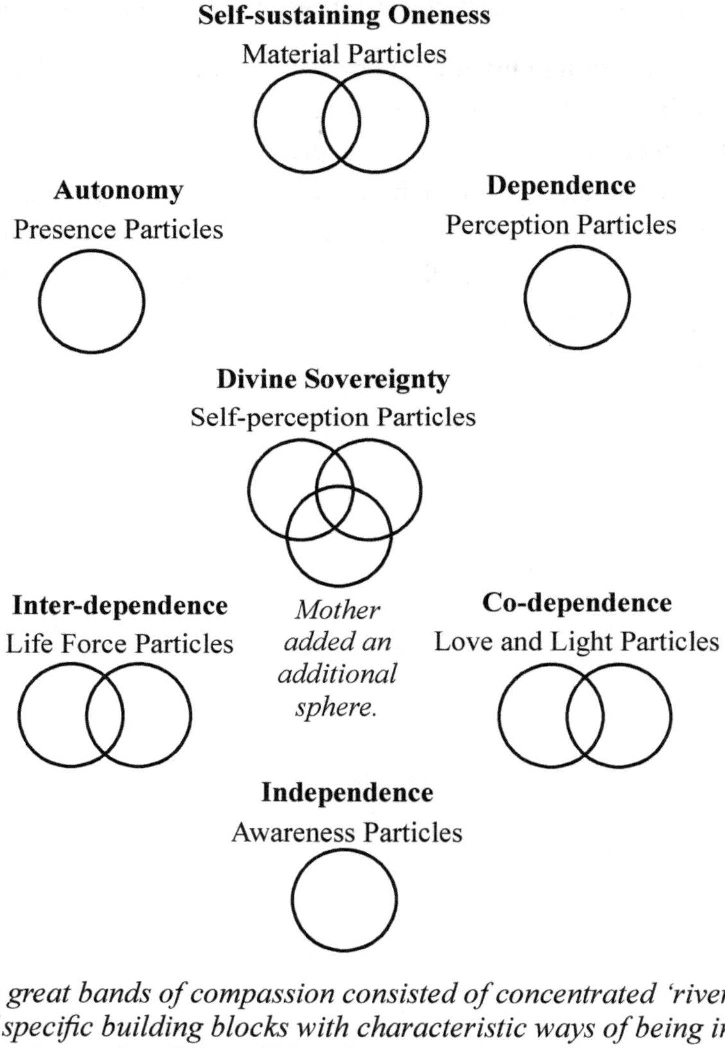

Self-sustaining Oneness
Material Particles

Autonomy
Presence Particles

Dependence
Perception Particles

Divine Sovereignty
Self-perception Particles

Inter-dependence
Life Force Particles

Mother added an additional sphere.

Co-dependence
Love and Light Particles

Independence
Awareness Particles

The great bands of compassion consisted of concentrated 'rivers' of specific building blocks with characteristic ways of being in relationship. When all but the material particles became omni-particles, there were only two bands of compassion left; Self-sustaining Oneness and Omnipresence.

Figure 3

The Building Blocks and the Bands of Compassion

Excerpt from *Windows into Eternity*

1. **Dependence (Perception Particles):** The function of the perception particles is entirely dependent on outer mirrors. It is also dependant on having that which is perceived already existing within its database, or else it cannot compute what it sees in the external mirrors.

2. **Co-Dependence (Love and Light Particles):** These particles have an internal co-dependence in that they depend on each other's contribution, i.e. empathy and telepathy, to have understanding. Furthermore, co-dependence tries to understand the unfamiliar by embracing it within the familiar. This is exactly what these particles do to embrace the unfamiliar with compassionate understanding.

3. **Independence (Awareness Particles):** Awareness particles are very much concerned with self-exploration. The individuation is explored vis-à-vis its role regarding other individuations. The self learns about itself by observing how it fits into the big picture. Being self-aware means that the main focus is the self, independent of whether there are other beings or not.

4. **Interdependence (Life Force Particles):** All particles that are double circles are masculine, versus those that consist of one sphere. That means that although both love and light are present, light is expressing more dominantly. The one mind of interdependence expresses by means of this prevalent light.

5. **Autonomy (Presence Particles):** The presence particles are feminine, being one sphere, and express frequency dominantly even though they contain an intermingled field of light and love. Autonomy is diversity within unity, oneness of heart with diverse thoughts. All is changed without by changing within, and thereby affecting the unified field of the one heart.

6. **Divine Sovereignty (Self-Perception Particles):** Divine sovereignty forms a oneness both through the heart and through the mind (light). This relationship is formed within, between its own components, and without with the other particles.

7. **Self-Sustaining Oneness (Material Particles):** The omni-particles that resulted from all previous particles combined are in self-sustaining oneness with the material particles – an immovable relationship that creates the power necessary for manifestation.

Almine's Note: The relationship of the building blocks here given, is for the seven directions of Lower Consciousness only. The lower level of consciousness functions from seven directions and the Higher Consciousness from eight, as seen by comparing their sub-personalities.

The two axes of existence that the lower levels of consciousness are based on have four directions that face away from the central source. This means that the other four directions that have their points touching the central source when they are folded over into an arc (creating a tube torus shape) are intermediaries for the other four. They have to obtain and translate messages of Infinite intent. The same is true for the building blocks – numbers 5 to 8 are the interpreters of the Infinite's intent.

The configuration of the axes for higher consciousness allows the direct input to occur. The records say:

> *Melechba nesurat aresh vivechspri minuhes upavuva.*
> The only language in existence is that of Divine Intent.

Book I – The Science of Peace

The symbol for the axes of higher consciousness is a spider, indicating that the human has passed through the gate of Arakana to a higher level of existence – a different reality. It also has eight legs operated by the body (the Embodiment).

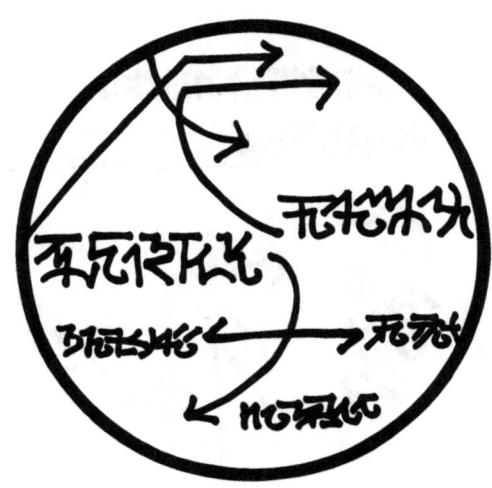

In the lower axes, four of the legs would not be working properly because they are not being instructed directly by the spider's body but by the other legs. The reception of a 'leg' or direction is done by the feminine, receptive pole. The interpretation and output is done by the electrical, masculine. They speak different languages.

Book I – The Science of Peace

According to the records of Ananu, the axes of lower consciousness have a story the way each human has a story.

Kavanechvi arsarat ubichve haruvarstat.
The Inner Babe had wandered into the center.

Piharana iklesh Mananu karetvi harubarstat. Isete manuch eseve kiranet.
The Embodiment of the Infinite went to look for the little one who was crying.

Mesetach aresh isanat pirekvi harubarstat. Ista vanesh plivech irekve manusa esekla.
The bright light of the center was scorching him. She did not notice where he was.

Virska plahech aresta pra-usana klivesva. Virabach spararet uselena.
She wandered into the spinning tube torus in her search. There was great forgetfulness.

Persa nunes u-arakana miset haruhus vireskla piret. Kirarut sekve virskave usuratvi mananut.
When once more the portal of Arakana again opens. Then shall the child be found.

Sinach haresta klahuvavechvi hersanat.
He shall be put in his proper rest place.

Kisarut ereska vabri estachve Manuhit arskachve uklesh vabrit vinesvi.
Then shall the Embodiment take Her place upon the throne and direct life.

The Facets of Wise Woman

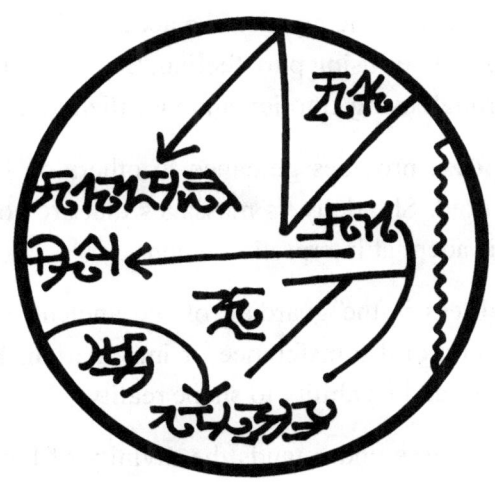

Excerpt from *A Life of Miracles*

The Thirteen Goddess Archetypes

The First Goddess forms a bridge with other life forms. She has reverence for all life; therefore, she remains sensitive to the interactions between all beings. She can hear nature speaking and is in harmony with its cycles because she feels them within her.

The Second Goddess is the history keeper. She knows the history of people is kept in their bones and the history of the earth is kept in stones. She remembers and preserves history to ensure that the energetic channels of the earth, the leylines, remain open and flowing.

The Third Goddess uses her innate sense of justice to measure actions. She makes sure all beings are treated fairly. She will defend the helpless and vulnerable.

The Fourth Goddess is the mystic. She accesses information through non-cognitive processes using pure feeling. She is the intuitive and she alters reality through using emotion and visualization.

The Fifth Goddess provides guidance to others on how their life's purpose will unfold. She delivers messages that are coming from the ancestors. She is adept at interpreting omens.

The Sixth Goddess is the guardian of the ancient, sacred tradition of story-telling and oral transference of information. She honors the power of the word and its ability to shape reality.

The Seventh Goddess understands the divinity of beauty and grace. She adds warmth and sensuality to life. She is the homemaker and takes care of the needs of the family. She loves without judgement.

The Eighth Goddess is in charge of death and birth. She works with herbs and communicates directly with the spirits of the plants used for medicinal purposes. She is a healer and knows the use of ritual.

The Ninth Goddess feels how actions will influence upcoming generations. She leaves them a heritage that nurtures growth.

The Tenth Goddess is the artist and muse. She is spontaneously creative about finding solutions. She inspires others.

The Eleventh Goddess honors the self. She promotes self-respect through praise. She nurtures individuality in herself and others.

The Twelfth Goddess celebrates accomplishments and designs ceremony. She lives in a state of praise.

The Thirteenth Goddess is the door of everything[3]. She forms a passageway into Godhood through stillness of being. She is the guardian of the keys that unlock the gate between the known and the unknown. When all the other archetypes are expressing harmoniously together, she takes charge of the alchemical processes that will alter the body to prepare it for ascension.

---

3 See *Odes of Solomon.*

The Facets of the Inner Sage

Excerpt from *A Life of Miracles*

The Twelve God Archetypes

The First God analyzes how mankind can sustain the race with the help of nature without disturbing its balance. He deals with earth sciences and analyzes what will enhance the productivity of the earth. He understands electromagnetic fields and how they respond to the sacred spaces and locations on earth.

The Second God gathers information about the known and analyzes the lessons from past experiences. He knows history from geology and archaeology. He learns lessons from ancient civilizations.

The Third God is the protector of the boundaries of individuals and society. He is the policeman and judge, making sure the boundaries are set and enforced.

The Fourth God analyzes the spiritual laws that govern the universe. His quest is to see symbolically and understand the truths hidden behind the illusions and symbols.

The Fifth God analyzes the hidden challenges within problems. He gathers insights from experiences. He prepares strategies to overcome weaknesses.

The Sixth God is a teacher. He allows students to learn through their own experiences. He devises analogies, metaphors and parables to assist people into effortlessly learning. He sees the value of humor in teaching techniques.

The Seventh God discerns how compassion should be expressed to best benefit the recipient. He ensures that his loved ones are respectfully treated. He analyzes and nurtures weak areas of relationships.

The Eighth God is responsible for male initiations and rites of passage. He works with the study of medicine, anatomy, botany and pharmacy.

The Ninth God is a goal setter. He measures progress by goals achieved. He possesses a strong survival instinct.

The Tenth God is a creative problem solver. He is the inventor who pushes limited vision beyond its boundaries.

The Eleventh God forges new paths to fulfill the yearnings of the heart. He provides leadership and endurance and is the guardian of impeccability.

The Twelfth God is the architect of pomp and splendor and creates order by developing hierarchy.

Whereas the spinning tube torus has generated energy and resources for the center, the higher reality has Creation (the tube torus) being fed by the center (the Embodiment of the Infinite).

Kanavash pirirat uklesbi haruret karesh vavi.
Linear change shall yield to exponential unfoldment

The tube torus is linear time. The center is the fluid eternal moment.

Overcoming the Hold of the Past

Stepping into Freedom

Men say that they search for truth, but they are searching for confirmation of already held belief systems, making their prison bars thicker and thicker.

Almine

The Prison Bars of Man

The cage of time and space, the tube torus, may be said to be the biggest prison bars of existence. But not so. Time and space were formed by an even bigger tyrant: a belief system.

The first belief that formed was that a question could exist, and secondly that there could be an answer anywhere. Belief systems handed down from generation to generation ensnare authentic expression and enslave the mind.

Belief systems create worldviews that give us blind spots in our awareness. From these blind spots, personalities and ego-identification form. Personalities are behavior patterns and programs that become entrenched in the psyche and dictate our choices and actions.

We can never call ourselves free while programs of any kind stifle the innocence of our being and the value systems of others run our lives. It requires ruthless diligence with ourselves to eliminate these programs. Ways to assist us with setting ourselves free include:

1. Slow life down by allowing several minutes every two hours to just be. Just sit at your desk or in your home and allow all thoughts to melt away. This is different than meditation. It is mindlessness.

2. Cultivate the practice of knowing the origin of your actions. Living meaningfully, deliberately and deeply will increasingly become a way of life.

3. Habitually take time to be alone. This slows life down. Empty the mind and just observe life. Refrain from making value judgements about what you experience.

4. Flow like a river through your day without getting attached to any part of it. Observe all encounters the way the travelling river

would see the riverbanks passing by - without agenda or value judgements.

The act of removing ourselves from the belief systems that create the bonds for tribes will inevitably lead to the dissolving of some of the more meaningless groups around you. Others, like families that bring you joy, will go through stages of evolving to a higher reality. It is inevitable. One cannot change without changing everything in our environment.

Once we have risen in consciousness beyond the masses by removing much of our belief systems – a never-ending process – tolerance with others is required. The games, cords and entanglements stand starkly revealed. Your mind becomes still as the thoughts that maintained the belief systems die away.

Firstly, we must remember that each note in a symphony is important – even the silent ones. It is in seeing the value of an illusion that it can finally yield to a higher order. The values of belief systems in the lives of the masses are:

1. Like the riverbanks, they confine the flow of life, but they also guide it on its winding way until eventually reaching the ocean. In this way they serve as a timing mechanism of awakening.

2. The riverbanks give stability to growth. Belief systems that are too suddenly removed can produce shock and regression as the unprepared person reaches for the stability of obsolete ways. Allow others their realities, unless they truly reach for your assistance. All we can do is inspire and guide them to ask the right question. The answers for our reality are not the same as for theirs. Trying to 'fix' their lives assumes that anything could be imperfect. Life is eternal and we play many different roles upon its eternal stage.

Responding to Negativity without Getting into a Savior Mode

When we enter a life of no opposites we realize we are a unified, indivisible field. Each life is a specific emphasis within that field, the way multiple ingredients make a cake. But all is indivisible; inseparately connected.

The only beneficial changes we can make in another's life is through changing ourselves. Ours is after all the only reality we can access and influence.

Find what they mirror and locate it in yourself. We attract mirrors that inspire us by showing us what we have yet to learn about ourselves or have lost along the way. We attract likewise mirrors of what we are or what we judge.

The most insidious flaws that come to bind our awareness are self-importance and self-pity. With humility, let us therefore remind ourselves that the lives of others are seen through a series of mirrors. Mirrors give back to front images. What looks back to front in our reality and from our perspective may not seem so in another's reality. Let us therefore not strengthen another's self-pity with our self-important advice, but in humility acknowledge the perfection of life. Only in this way can we stay free from the ties that bind.

The Mystical Relationships of the Cosmos

The three stages of linear change have a mystical relationship that feed off one another. The understanding of them will assist us in clearly seeing the dynamics of our own relationships. This will help us avoid being caught in another form of treadmill and its self-perpetuating motion.

The Anatomy of Change

Excerpt from *Journey to the Heart of God*

As awareness moves outward through the cosmos in spiralling arcs, our lives move with it. The cycles in our lives are linked to the cycles of the spirals. There are small cycles within large ones. The only constant we encounter in life is that everything changes; awareness always moves.

As we go through either the smaller changes in our lives or the larger more dramatic ones, a pattern starts to emerge; a map we can use to identify what stage of change we are in. Each cycle goes through three distinct phases, identifiable by their symptoms.

Transformation

As we grow in awareness and problems are recognized for what they truly are (opportunities for growth), they lose their hold on us and we no longer need them. Suddenly circumstances in our lives seem to change. Friendships fall by the wayside, jobs may become obsolete and we find life flowing a lot more effortlessly as it transforms before our eyes.

This stage is marked by so many changes that it can be called the time of the death of the old. If we hold on longer than we should to relationships or situations, we find life shedding them for us through forced change. This time can certainly be disconcerting as the old platform we stood on disintegrates, but the energy released when that which no longer serves us drops away, is a great reward. With increased energy comes new experiences and ease in meeting old challenges that bring a sense of deep self-satisfaction. As one sheds the old, the body responds by purifying itself. Toxins release and the body can hold more light.

Transmutation

After transformation sheds the unnecessary parts of our lives, the true challenges stand revealed. This phase is the one where most people get stuck. Mindlessly feeling victimized by the very experiences their higher selves designed for them, they fail to turn pain to wisdom, judgements to compassion. The very essence of transmutation is to turn something of a lower frequency into a higher frequency; the alchemical process of turning lead to gold.

During the phase of transmutation, we are confronted with never before encountered challenges or those we have failed to learn from. Life has just served the ball across the net and waits for our response. The harder the serve, the more we can gain. More people spend their whole life running away from the balls coming across the net instead of hitting them back.

If we can find the lessons and insights of our challenges, we score enough points to move on to the next game. If we are very diligent, we can even gain insights on behalf of others, increasing our points on the scoreboard. The insights we gain during this stage must be tested to turn them into experiential knowledge.

Transfiguration

Major transfigurations, such as disconnecting from ego-identification (becoming God-conscious) and entering into Immortal Mastery, come but a few times in one's life. All change however, follows this exact map with its three stages. The largest transfigurations are just more noticeable. Even the little ones add up, eventually allowing enough light into our lives for our entire life to transfigure. As more and more clarity is gained, the person must transfigure in order to accommodate the increased light.

The joyous truth is that there is no end to progression. When we have made it through all the evolutionary stages of man's awareness, we shall move even beyond that ultimate goal of humanness: Immortal Mastery. Beyond lies the god kingdom where we can come and go with the speed of thought throughout all realms of time and space – the cosmos is our playground.

The Relationship Between Cosmoses

The study of the fields around the body of man have revealed that there are three each of various geometric forms that are stacked inside one another like Russian dolls. The three star-tetrahedrons are all occupying the same space. One spins counter-clockwise (electrical), one spins clockwise (magnetic – for realities of lower consciousness, the feminine spins slower) and one is stationary. This is the same for all subsequent shapes.

Around the star-tetrahedrons there are octahedrons (four-sided pyramids base to base) and then dodecahedrons (consisting of spheres of pentagons, like a soccer ball). Around and through all of these are the 3 tube toruses. The cosmoses, of which there are three, can be considered the fields around the Infinite's Embodiment.

We have been speaking about our cosmos, a spinning field that folds outward and then rolls over its edge to fold inward. It is however the electric one of the three. It is occupying the same space as the magnetic one and the neutral one. The cells of our bodies reflect the same trinity.

But unlike the other shapes within it, the three are not identical in appearance or movement. The neutral one consists of a rapidly spinning ring (spinning opposite to our cosmos) with a saucer-shaped (two saucers inverted on top of each other) field within it. The saucer flips over and back at regular intervals, alternating between receptivity and proactivity.

The third cosmos is feminine and consists of very refined ethereal matter we cannot detect. It has the ability to lower its frequency during cycles of contraction. The entire cosmos vacillates between expansion and implosions (big bangs and black holes).

The loss of resources during the expansion, catapults it into contraction during which it falls into the realities below – that of the other two cosmoses. Both a big bang and an implosion into a black hole strips the resources through which it moves.

Since this cosmos enters ours during the implosion phase, it takes our resources and sucks them through the black hole into the reality it came from – stealing our building blocks of life like a vampire.

In the writings of the ancient Records of Ananu, the three cosmoses are called: the clown (ours), the juggler (the neutral one) and the thief (the feminine one).

The same relationships are prevalent in our lives. Their aim is to hook you into the middle of their games so that you can become a source of empowering them. The Infinite cannot be embodied in the middle of cosmic life – it is an imagined role. The ocean cannot be contained within the island, yet the island is in the ocean and the ocean is in the island.

Relationship Types that Ensnare
The Clown

The traditions of the Norse people had Loki as the trickster. In Native American traditions he is called Hay-ho-ka, the sacred clown. In the tarot, it is the jester. The game of this personality type has the subtle agenda to keep you off balance and thus keep them in control. They are like a loose cannon – you never know where you will be embarrassed or shocked or defensive next. They pride themselves in their 'honesty' and their 'spontaneity' but their indiscriminate, undisciplined speech is designed to attract attention through startling us.

Shock and surprise causes a loss of power and energy. The Earth's cataclysms have almost always resulted in a fall of consciousness, since consciousness requires energy and an accumulation of personal power to sustain it.

People with this personality profile suck the energy up by being the center of your attention as you release resources by being taken by surprise.

The Juggler

The dynamics are the same as for the Clown in that as you focus on their games, your surprise and shock release resources they benefit from. They are the ones who imbalance you through unpredictable mood swings and rages.

There is little rationale for the sudden outbursts and the roller-coaster ride of their emotions. This instability makes it impossible to see the tantrums or rages coming, thus we are taken by surprise and drained by the experience.

The shock becomes all the more devastating because their need to keep you from abandoning them due to their rages, drives them into being particularly caring and giving in between the periods of abusiveness. We believe the latter to be their 'real' self and the rages something they can overcome. Because we open up to them during their loving, ingratiating periods, the rage causes an even greater shock, allowing them to suck up even more power and energy.

Neither part of their conduct is 'real' in that they do not represent who they could be if they lived authentically from their core, since both parts are based on controlling your responses to them.

People who are over-polarized into the masculine or feminine, are particularly prone to this unstable behavior because they are not supported by a firm foundation; their own inner feminine or masculine components. They fluctuate between self-importance and self-pity, whereas the clown has mostly self-importance and the thief operates from self-pity.

The Thief

The thief is subversive and never openly engages you. They come across as helpful, friendly and caring. They have their own way of getting your attention so that they can be empowered. They are masters at benefitting from the law that we empower what we focus on.

The range of behavior with this and the other personalities varies widely from the subtle to the more obvious and overt: at the subtle end is the ignorance and helplessness act. You explain something simple and even though they understand, multiple questions follow to hook your attention. If you do not pay your 'dues' by engaging in their game, it is done incorrectly because you 'did not explain it properly'. This personality type wants to stay connected with you at any cost; after all they have deliberately chosen you for your high ability to be their power source. They forget an item in your car or house so that you have to mail or bring it to them – more attention extracted from you.

The slightly more aggressive thief will provide you with competent assistance. In fact they will create within you, a deliberate dependency on them by doing more and more for you. Because they are rooted in self-pity, they do not feel lovable and instead settle for being needed. Many healers and psychics fit in this category. They are invigorated by the passion and fullness of another's life.

The fact that they have so little (power, success, recognition, money, popularity, etc.) and you have so much, eventually causes behind-your-back destructiveness. They talk about you to others that are eager to hear, or put you in an unfavorable light, creating an even larger number of eager ears. They eventually undermine your business, reputation and finances.

The personality of the thief is based on the very first stage of social evolution, the dependency of the infant or child. This develops due to insufficient parenting. The juggler often experiences alcoholic or fighting parents. They feel uncomfortable in situations without the high tension of conflict, having become addicted to stress. They create stress and then feel angry that they are stressed. They also use stress as an excuse for their anger. They are co-dependant and follow its high-tension journey of stress that repeats over and over again:

1. *I love and support you.*
2. *Because of how much I give, I am privileged so I can control you.*
3. *If you don't meet my expectations, I am furious.*

The clown is independent. Its spinning and rolling tube torus is exuding a centrifugal force that pushes anything that is trying to connect with it away. If one tries to interact from the heart in an authentic way, they throw up a wall with an inappropriate response that sends you reeling.

The integrated person acts from interdependency. The low tension, high productivity stage, in which people come together, based on a common vision, instead of needs based on deficiencies. This stage supports individual expression and honors voluntary agreements of mutual contribution with the understanding that if it no longer makes someone's heart sing to be part of it, they are joyfully released from participating. This relationship is based on voluntary roles, rather than imprisoning dependencies.

The Trout

The trout swims upstream. If everyone is gathered together to create a holy ceremony, the trout will disrupt it. They argue when there is agreement and attract attention by swimming against the intent of the group.

The trout is not a team player and in singling themselves out, they get the attention of the many. We empower what we focus on. This becomes an addictive habit by the trout, in that there is always a 'fix' of energy and resources coming his or her way that reinforces their tendency to do antisocial and disruptive things.

Social and Relationship Stages

Excerpt from *Journey to the Heart of God*

The evolutionary stages of relationship are the same for interpersonal or cultural relationship.

1. **Dependence:** In this stage similarities are stressed. Couples experience this as their initial stages of being 'in love'. They feel euphoric because they see themselves in the mirror of the other person. Culturally this manifests as tribal life where the individual is expected to behave in a certain way in exchange for the tribe's support.

2. **Co-dependency:** Some individuality is expressed, but there is still a strong desire to identify with each other and no-one steps too far out of 'the box'. Many tribal members in North America are in this stage, where they live in the city, but retain strong ties of dependence with the tribe.

3. **Independence:** In personal interaction each individual becomes almost desperate to find his or her own identity. Differences now become emphasized. In the modern, mechanized societies all types of insurance are needed since there is no tribal support. In apartments people live without knowing their neighbor's name.

4. **Interdependence:** If stage 3 can be survived, this stage brings more stability. The individuals are secure in their relationships, and supportive of each other's differences. This is the template for communal living for the future: a group lives together because of a common goal, voluntarily commits certain contributions and is free to express and grow in diversity.

The Four Stages of Conflict Resolution

Excerpt from *Journey to the Heart of God*

Conflict resolution also mirrors the evolving of awareness. It moves through conflict to evolved awareness through the same four distinct stages.

Stage 1

In the Primary Trinity, the I AM gathers all that is uploaded to it from the insights of our lives, all new information about the mystery of beingness. But within the Infinite the same poles attract and within Creation opposite poles attract. The Primary Trinity, therefore, attracts all that resonates the same. In other words, it keeps and grows more luminous from that which it recognizes to be the same, namely that which is life enhancing. The rest is passed on to the Creative Trinity for resolution.

In the first stage of resolution, we find our common ground. Unless this is first identified we cannot properly determine which parts to resolve in Stage 2. Failure to determine what we have in common with the opposition robs us of the priceless gift of becoming more knowledgeable by learning new aspects and viewpoints of that which we are (common ground). Too often, opponents prematurely focus on the differences during this first stage instead of simply assimilating the commonalities so that these initial gifts of insight can be received.

Stage 2

The Creative Trinity, having received all parts the I AM did not recognize as resonating similarly, now engages in analysis, weighing the unknown pieces against all that has been previously known. Once again it gathers to itself all that can be found to be the same (life enhancing), examines it in a larger context and isolates that which is different. It now tackles the solving of these unknown pieces through externalizing them through Creation.

In this stage of conflict resolution a closer scrutiny of what is the same and what is different must take place. Those unknown pieces must be examined in depth, rather than taken at face value to extract common elements. It is necessary to examine these details in the context of the larger picture. Although we may have superficial differences, are we exploring a similar pattern? Are the core issues the same even though our method in dealing with them might be different? In this way the true differences to resolve are isolated from the similarities.

The last step is to creatively externalize them. Design a case scenario – objectively examine the issues as though they are happening to someone else. Reverse roles, honestly examining what it would be like to be in the other person's shoes.

Stage 3

Within the Trinity of Indwelling Life, opposites attract. The known (light), no longer pushes the unknown away, but instead desires to incorporate it within. It wants to turn the unknown into the known through experience. For this it needs form and so must create materialization.

In conflict resolution this stage requires that we abandon our preoccupation with our own viewpoint and genuinely try to understand the opposing position. The need now arises to create a situation to test the validity of the opposing viewpoint, to see and understand it better by observing it is action. Where the stakes are high, the testing of the unknown can be done in multiple, smaller controlled settings.

- Your teenager wants to date. You feel she's too young, she feels you're ruining her life because all her friends date. After completing the previous steps, one or two controlled situations could be tested wherein she is dropped off and picked up by you and has to call you if she changes locations. This option is opposed to one requiring an absolute yes or no with one party or the other feeling unheard. An informed conclusion can then be drawn as to what can be supported.

Stage 4

In the Trinity of Materialization, the unknown is incorporated into the known through experience. The previously unknown parts of the Infinite's being become known through our experiencing them and taking the time to gain the insights those experiences yield. New knowledge is gained.

In this stage we agree to disagree. The level of interaction is determined by what can be assimilated without being destructive to inner life or without being light and growth repressive. The key element of the success of this stage is to keep supporting the areas of common ground and the growth of all. Examples of the different degrees of interaction that could be allowed are:

- The in-laws don't like you but they love your wife. Because they show their dislike when around you, you needn't be in their presence often but nevertheless support your spouse being with them as she chooses. If their intent is destructive, such as to break up the marriage, this needs to be clearly identified and the interaction must then be very minimal or terminated depending on the accompanying level of risk.
- If differences are only superficial but the common goals and philosophies are strong, we find we can live closely together or work together while honoring and supporting our diversity within our unity.

As we have moved through these stages, we have encountered the following ways of relating to each other.

Uniformity: This is the stage of dependence on sameness to understand ourselves more fully.

Co-dependence: Exploring sameness versus difference – co-dependence is experienced as we find sameness in the differences. We understand ourselves by observing that which we are not.

Independence: In exploring differences we seek our independence by focusing on that which we are not as mirrored by the other party. We determine whether the relationship is worth proceeding with.

Interdependence: Unity within diversity is the stage of interdependence where we cooperate for the good of the common goals, supporting the diversity each contributes.

This final stage is the goal of all life since it provides the greatest opportunity for growth, whereas uniformity slows growth through stagnation. The more differences there are, the more uncomfortable the relationship will be; the greater the commitment to the greater goal, the more stable.

The Deeper Mysteries of Existence

Part II

The Records of Ananu

Keresh pa uhuru nechspi arat paravi asakle
Know now the body, for illusion begins there

Arsa-ranatve iraklesh harustat pirane uvilavespe huranet
The vastness of cosmoses is but the reflection of the cells

Book I – The Science of Peace

The heart knows not its rhythm.
It pumps to hear its breath...

Christina, USA

From the records:
The senses were developed as life unfolded through its stages of evolution. First sight came about as a mirror developed from the first question, and relationship began.

The next sensory perception came through hearing as the first outward movement began. But like the images in the mirror, the lines curved and through this arcing movement, the tube torus was born.

Questions consist of dark light and answers consist of white light. Dark light holds potential and white light is accessed information. All light eventually arcs because the nature of light seeks to return to its source of origin.

The first cell to develop from which life was formed is a heart cell. The first sound to be heard is the pumping of the heart cell. The body of our cosmos (the tube torus) had a first cell from which all others came – the Earth.

Almine's Note: Many records from several hidden libraries have indicated that life began on Earth. The Lemurian Records of Life and Death call the Earth:

> *Panu Arukna Veresh*
> The Cradle of Civilization

The word **Pana** or **Pan** is often used as the root for the word Earth in ancient languages.

Book I – The Science of Peace

The Earth pulsates like a heartbeat through the cosmos. The tube torus of the cosmos lies around the Earth as its center. Where the outward and inward movement of the vast cosmic tube torus begins, is where the central little sun (called Klanivik) of the Earth lies.

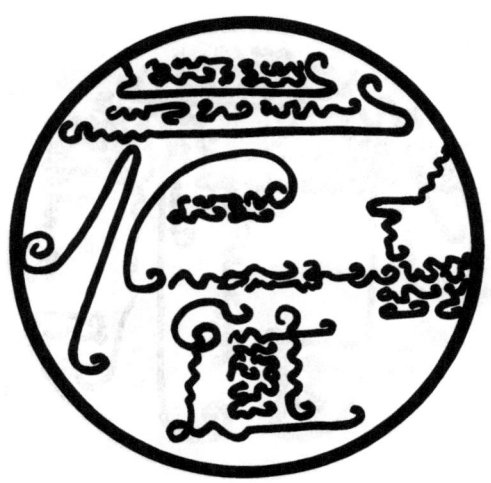

The dominance of the outward movement (the red road away from the heart or arterial system) alternates with the dominance of the inward movement (the blue road back to the heart or venous system). In polarity, for every movement there is an opposite and equal movement that follows. One pushes, the other pulls back. This is why the cosmos rolls out and in, and because these opposites meet inside the Earth, why the Earth beats.

Almine's Note: Earth and heart have the same letters in English, the 'h' simply needs to move from the beginning to the end of the word. The music I received from Source for the in-breath and out-breath of the Earth's central sun is called Klanivik I and Klanivik II and is available on the music CD, *Children of the Sun*.

Book I – The Science of Peace

When living a reality that is dictated by the caged movement of the tube torus and the linear time that it forms, we feel as though we can never get ahead because every step forward, creates a step backwards somewhere else in our life. This has caused depression, which is rage turned inward. The depression of the creatures in the cosmos has caused self-destructiveness or recklessness; the two key components of the Clown.

The shape of the tube torus is formed by what the ancients call *Isanva* or *Isangva*. This means 'the silver serpents of heaven'. These are the ropes of awareness: the DNA of the cosmos. These serpents or ropes are what drives life along its course, which is predetermined by the tube torus. They are formed by life force particles and are called the animating factor of the flow of life. This also means that they are the root of time, which is movement within a designated space.

Man is the root race; the most dense, but the most complex being in expression. Man is the microcosmic archetype of the macrocosm. Man's DNA is polluted by an encrusted layer of debris: the ancestral programming of past generations and the old experiential belief systems of past incarnations.[4] If this is the case for humanity, the same must be true for cosmic DNA: the spirals of awareness. (See Figure 4: The Three Types of Awareness.)

---

4 *Shrihat Satva Yoga* is specifically designed to clear past life programming.

The debris in the cosmic DNA comes from previous in- and out-breaths of the tube torus. It lies in ghostly patterns of black light (unanswered questions) called grids. It becomes stuck to the strands of awareness in the following way:

1. Awareness does not move when we live in full surrender, which puts us in timelessness. We accomplish this by being fully present for ourselves every moment and completely aware in the moment.

2. If we abandon parts of our authentic self-expression and resist life, it creates porous 'holes' in the awareness spirals allowing old programs in. As with all else, self-abandonment and lack of presence creates invasion and pollution.

When we are not aware in this moment, awareness creates a counterfeit, artificial substitute – the future moment (something that is a complete illusion) to move to instead, and the movement of awareness begins. It moves in search of a moment in which we are present. Life always tries to fill what is empty, the way the ocean fills any hole we attempt to make in it.

By ceasing to oppose life and by being fully aware of the wonderment of the moment, we can shed the dust of the ages that brings about limitation by polluting our DNA. Instead of every generation becoming more steeped in illusion, by gathering more and more old programming in their DNA, we can evolve the species beyond the limitation of the tube torus. It begins with refusing to live a programmed life. Only then can we enter a life of no opposites; a field of indivisibility in which we can design and unfold our own unique waveform of jubilation.

The Three Types of Awareness

Excerpt from *Journey to the Heart of God*

Original Awareness
Movement: It arcs
Originates: Within the Spirit Body
Polarity: Neutral
Location: It moves through all 7 bodies

Inherent Awareness
Movement: A straight line
Originates: Within the Mental Body
Polarity: Masculine
Location: It moves through the 4 lower bodies

Evolving Awareness
Movement: It spirals
Originates: Within the Physical Body
Polarity: Feminine
Location: It moves through the physical body

The three types of awareness create the tube torus of the Infinite and its Creation. It consists of trillions of arcing spirals propelling away from and returning to Source or originating point.

Figure 4

Learning to Live with Diversity

*Like a play that now has passed
That the audience can contemplate at last
Learn to value what once was
That you can dissolve the illusions
of the past*

The Saradesi Records

The Seven Bodies of Man in the Lower Realities

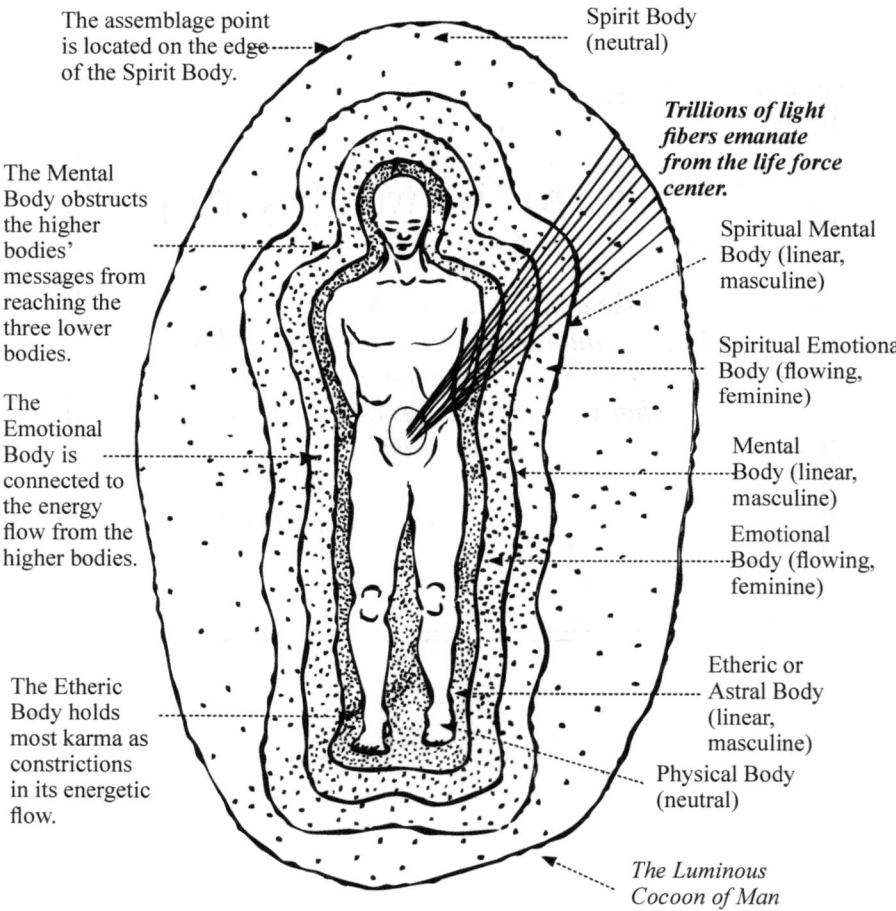

The bodies are superimposed over each other and form the luminous cocoon of man. The trillions of light fibers from the life force center penetrate all other bodies, forming the spirit body.

Figure 5

Chakras of Those in Identity–Consciousness

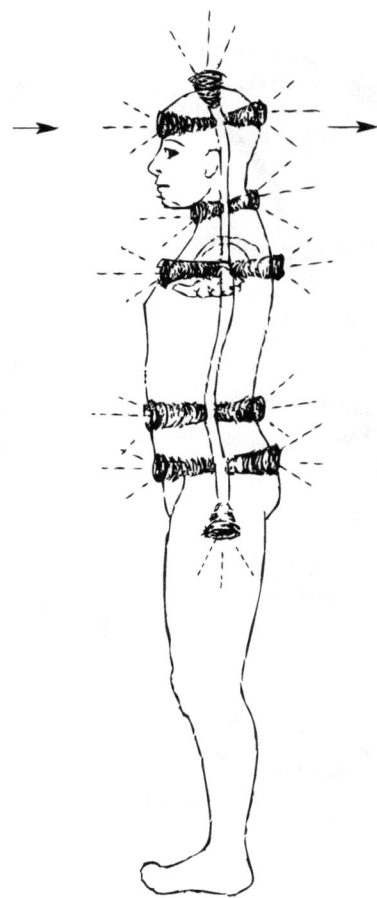

Seven levels of light enter the chakras. It cannot immediately assimilate and download into the endocrine system because of the blockages and acidic pH present. This occurs in the cells of a person who hasn't overcome the past and holds on to that which no longer serves.

Figure 6

The Seed of Life

Figure 7

The Wheel of the One Life
The Screen

Figure 8

Understanding the Differences

The Essene Scrolls state that a time would come when two different grids (matrices) would exist on Earth. That they would dictate and facilitate two different realities has now come to pass. They speak of the ones who would walk between the worlds; the ones who are of the higher realities assisting to ease life in the lower realities by bringing understanding so that they may move on.

Only one who has left the confines of the fish bowl can, looking back, show others the way out.

Simon, Canada

The Lower Realities

- Those who live from this level are based on principles of transformation. They reject one pole in favor of the opposite pole. All their choices are based on what is life enhancing to them and what is not. They are in identity consciousness.
- They have only seven sub-personalities and their driving force is needs-based because their Inner Babe is the central personality.
- They have little inner guidance and make decisions based on outer guidance. The two main reasons for this are:

    1) The middle of their axes of experience is a two year old that is needy.

    2) Four of the seven sub-personalities are facing away from the center, leaving the Inner Warrior and Inner Nurturer to guide them.

- Because they only function from seven directions, they only have seven building blocks of life that are accessible to them.
- The chakras of the body are little vortices that receive information from the different building blocks of life. They then download it to the endocrine system that conveys it to the rest of the body as subtle information. They have only seven chakras. (See *Fig. 5 & 6*)
- The three star-tetrahedronal fields are the ones that predominantly determine this lower reality. There are three sides to each interlocking pyramid as well as the middle point: six around the seventh just like the sub-personalities.
- When a two dimensional circle (cell) wants to duplicate itself, it creates a seed of life – six identical circles that fit exactly around the identical seventh circle. If all circles are the same size, no matter what size they are, the 6 will fit around the 7th. The life of this reality is two dimensional. The reason it seems three-dimensional, is because it is on a 'television' screen – a flat wheel.
- The ability to feel a full range of emotions is very limited in two-dimensional life. When there is an absence of expression, artificial life takes its place. Anger, pain, fear, protectiveness and guilt are therefore everywhere in this lower reality where most live their daily lives. They are artificial emotions.
- Linear change, and its three components, is the way life unfolds in the lower reality. This creates linear time and disturbs their innocence. This in turn creates mind and a busy inner dialogue that makes true hearing impossible. Everyone is talking, but no-one can hear.
- Their brain waves are on a Beta (12 – 30 Hz) frequency. This is indicative of hyper, linear, addictive and memory-based living.
- Their cellular structure mirrors the three cosmoses. There are three types of cells; one type is immortal and has two hydrogen atoms that alternate in dominance – it can live and divide for thousand of years – the juggler. One is mortal and multiplies itself rapidly

during its short lifespan. It seems to lack the purpose and blueprint held by the immortal cells and randomly changes its action without seemingly having a direction – the clown. The unseen cells steal the resources from the other two cells – just the way the cosmos did, through implosions and explosions – the thief.
- Beings of this realm have a soul (juggler), spirit (thief) and body (clown). The body believes that it depends on the spirit and soul for its survival. The same tyrannies exist within the body, in that it believes that vital organs must function for the body to survive. The body is thus enslaved by tyrants.
- Pressure is required to generate the resources to sustain life because it depends on polarity rather than Source for continued existence.

The Higher Realities

- Those who are living from this level are based on principles of transmutation. They use the experiences of themselves and others as an energy and power source by converting them into perception. This also assists others in their evolution.
- They have eight sub-personalities directed by Source. Life has dynamic balance and is inspiration-based rather than need-based.
- This reality is less dense which permits questions and answers to be almost immediate, reducing the hold of the illusions of time and space. Living requires fewer resources, provides instant guidance in the form of automatic living, and unfolds with more grace.
- The eighth building block of undifferentiated intent enables them to receive and interpret guidance from Source. It places them in a state of god-consciousness.
- They have additional chakras. (See *Fig. 9*)

Book I – The Science of Peace

Transfiguration in the Chakra System

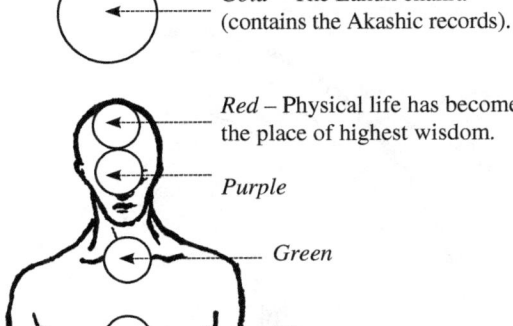

For descriptions of the Lahun chakra's specific function, see *The Ring of Truth.*

Gold – The Lahun chakra (contains the Akashic records).

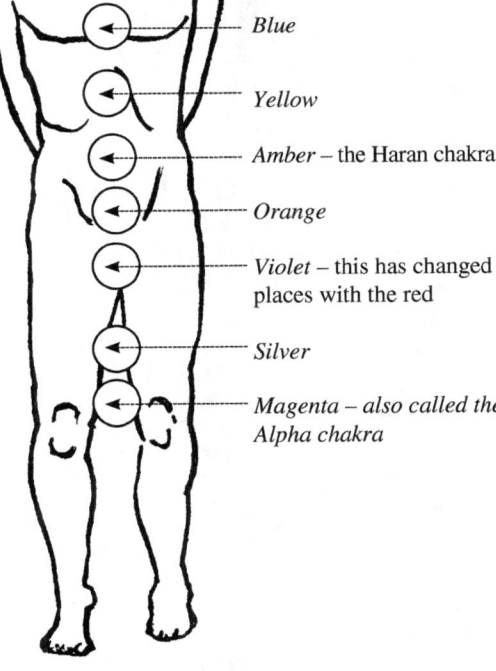

Red – Physical life has become the place of highest wisdom.

Purple

Green

Blue

Yellow

Amber – the Haran chakra

Orange

Violet – this has changed places with the red

Silver

Magenta – also called the Alpha chakra

The little known silver chakra contains a living library of earth history. Anciently called the Braamish chakra, the word Braamin comes from there.

Transfiguration in the body has also led to the same large changes taking place in the chakra system.

Figure 9

The Nine Bodies of Man
(Corresponding with the Nine Bodies of the Cosmos)

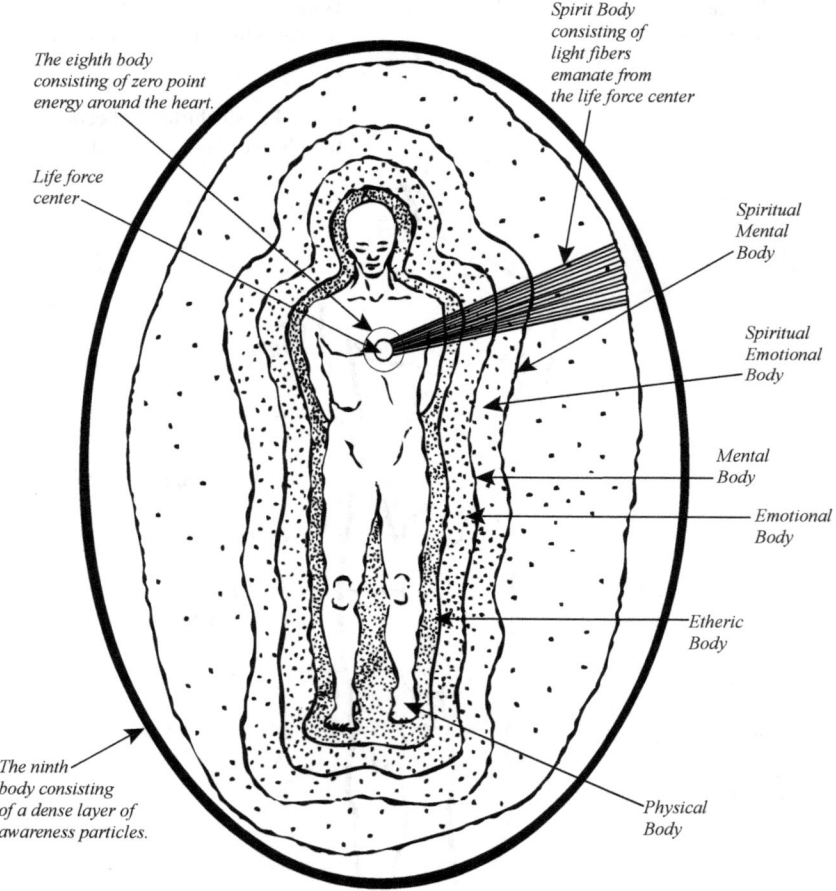

In April 2007, man's life force center was moved up from behind the belly button to the heart center. In May 2007, the cosmos, and man as the microcosm, received the eighth and ninth bodies. The eighth body consists of zero point energy around the heart chakra (now also surrounded by the small sphere of life force).

Figure 10

The Mystical Secrets of the Forgotten Chakras

Excerpt from *Windows into Eternity*

The Lahun Chakra

Depicted in ancient art and holy writings, a golden disc hovers above the heads of states and on images of holy ones. This disc, approximately 10 inches in diameter for most, is the golden colored Lahun chakra. Whereas the Haran chakra in the navel area is amber and the third chakra is bright yellow, the Lahun chakra is a true luminous gold color.

The Lemurian word for ten is 'lahun' meaning all in one and one in all. It is so named because during mastery's advanced stages, this Lahun or tenth chakra enlarges until it forms a large sphere reaching from just above the knees to about 2 feet above the head. At that point, the one is in all other chakras and all are in the one.

But the true glory of the Lahun chakra becomes active when a later most mystical union takes place: the union with the Braamish chakra.

The Braamish Chakra

The Braamish chakra is a beautiful silver color, usually about the same size as the other seven chakras. It is located about 2 inches below the perineum, or base of the spine. From the ancient libraries of the Butterfly, located in China, and opened for humanity by the Mother of all Life on February 2, 2008, comes more information:

From the 10th Scroll of the Blue Butterfly
> *"Inik glaava hurin peles pirit nisklavaa huvek. Setvilisk paranut skelevitvi usvrabaa..."*

"When libraries are opened and holy ones again dwell on Earth

When incorruptible white magic again is re-birthed
The secrets of the ages shall be released
And the Holy Mother shall begin a reign of peace"

***

"In a golden cocoon the silver butterfly is birthed
Holding within its heart the holy libraries of Earth"

The golden cocoon is the enlarged Lahun chakra and the 'silver butterfly' holding the secrets of the holy libraries in its heart is the Braamish chakra (Brahmin is derived from this term meaning 'Earth wisdom' in the Naga language, spoken in the mystery schools and temples of Lemuria. The word "Nagual' means one who officiated as a holy teacher). The preceding lines imply that some sort of birth takes place when the Lahun chakra enlarges enough to incorporate the silver Braamish one. The scroll continues in a later passage as follows:

"When the gold threads and the silver in a tapestry unite
When the flame of white magic through the two ignite
The birthright of man will be restored
On Earth, and more, a time of hope is born"

The Merging of the Gold and Silver Chakras

When the golden sphere of the Lahun chakra enlarges enough to incorporate the Braamish chakra, the latter is immediately sucked into the navel area, leaving its position at the base of the spine. Once there, it explodes into the golden orb of the enlarged Lahun chakra, forming a unified field. This merging (later in the scroll called the 'merging of heaven and Earth') brings about two enormous benefits:

1. The ancient libraries of wisdom become accessible. This means that the accumulated wisdom of the ages is at our disposal if we

take the time to listen within. The Lahun chakra holds the wisdom of the Akashic records. The Braamish chakra holds the wisdom of the sacred libraries.

2. The flame of white magic ignites. The depiction of the disc above the head in ancient murals often shows a cleft flame on either side of the disc. This is the awakened fire of the kundalini that causes a flame on top of the head. This is described in the New Testament as what the saints experienced at Pentecost. The power to do beneficial magic is directly proportional to how far up the spine the energy – also called the cold fire – can freely travel. This explosive merging clears blockages in the pranic tube and spinal column.

This mystical marriage and resulting alchemical reaction can be available to everyone. It is the culmination of deep self-exploration and the gaining of insights from experience. This removes blockages from the centers of the chakras until, at the apex of human experience, the sacred gifts of the Lahun and Braamish chakras await.

- The way has been prepared for years for this second higher reality to be lived on Earth. From the book *Opening the Doors of Heaven*, the following illustration is given of the nine bodies of man (Figure 10). Zero point energy is not the absence of particles or building blocks, such as what occurs when resources are stripped during implosions (black holes) or explosions (big bangs), but rather could be seen as a portal into Infinite Life that sustains us.
- The higher reality is based on octahedronal fields. This reality is more self-sustaining and has dynamic stability. The eight facets represent the 8 sub-personalities.
- The life of this reality is like a virtual reality hologram: three-dimensional. The body releases the stress of linear time by having stepped off the disc; out of the flat television screen. Life becomes

less pressured and more perspective is gained in observing the folly of others.
- The artificial emotions of fear, anger, protectiveness and pain become replaced by the 12 pairs of pure emotions. (See page 177.)
- Life unfolds exponentially and the gap between cause and effect closes. Many synchronicities occur to support their intent as separation consciousness diminishes. Life is lived in an eternal, fluid moment as resistance to life diminishes.
- Through a surrendered life, their brainwaves have a much lower frequency of Delta (0 – 4 Hz), enabling them to enter the still point and dissolve more illusions.
- Their cellular structure changes as the nucleus enlarges and a fourth cell, called the god-cell, emerges. This cell has been missing and in its absence, the cells have been acting independently rather than interdependently. With the presence of the god-cell, the body becomes able to transcend – fluidly regenerating itself into renewed expression. This state requires that we release belief systems.
- In relinquishing belief systems, the body is experienced as a field. There is neither a physical form nor a soul. An individuated formlessness, seen as 'spirit' does not exist. They see themselves as an emphasis within a unified field – therefore not separate from the rest of existence.
- Source is seen as something they dwell in and that dwells in them. They receive all resources necessary to sustain them, through this inclusiveness.

BOOK II

Freedom from the Treadmill

Introduction

Because of the in- and out-breaths of the cosmic tube torus, the unresolved issues of the lower reality accumulate: As it is with man, these traumatic unprocessed events and unanswered questions accumulate in the gaps between breaths.

If their insights are not gained, the tube torus does not smoothly roll over its edge and additional pressure is required in the form of cosmic or planetary cataclysms. In the lives of individuals or planets or cosmoses, this accounts for why significant events happen in cycles.

The division of two realities is part of the plan to help life unfold with ease and in a peaceful way transit between cosmic breaths. The lower reality is populated by beings that are the perception givers and the higher by perception getters.

The understanding that these are not identities of greater or lesser importance, but interdependent roles we play, contributes to the ease of life on Earth. The opposite is true if we try to save others rather than play our part well. This form of self-abandonment causes addiction of some sort within us, causing in turn stagnation.

When we stagnate, the lower realities are forced into a faster, hyperactive state. This reduces the ability for us and them to resolve issues in time to avert the necessity for cataclysms.

The higher realities hold the questions, the lower hold the answers. The interdependent cooperation to transition life into a smooth, peaceful unfolding, begins by honoring and appreciating one another's roles.

In the large tube toral field of the cosmos, we are entering the time of interdependency – the last stage before expansion becomes contraction. To go from one to the other, we need to cross the edge of the tube torus, where all unresolved conflicts are held.

The answer to averting catastrophes lies in getting the insights of what awaits in the gap between the breaths – before we get there. This can be done in one of two ways:

1. The Unpleasant Way – We increase our own hardship or that of others, in order to learn these insights more rapidly before cataclysms force us to.

2. The Pleasant Way – The easy way of learning what we missed, has always been through understanding our dreams and their symbolic messages to us. The previous cycles of cosmic life represent the dreams of the Embodiment of the Infinite. Being dreams, the part of the Infinite that enters the dreams to participate in them, is feminine: the Holy Mother Goddess.

The magnetic components of the building blocks of life hold the memory of these past cosmic dreams, The Cycles of Life. These memories form the Akashic Records.

Let us learn from them what is needed, that we may usher in a higher form of existence – a life wherein the questions and answers become one – a life of no opposites.

The History of the Cycles

The Wheel of the Opening of the Center of DNA

A Portal to Higher Creations

Introduction to the History of the Cycles

Throughout the eons of existence within our 'loop' of eighteen huge cycles, kingdoms have been subject to the vicissitudes of change. They have been part of rebellions, at times against Mother,[5] and at other times they have been attacked because they supported Her. They have changed leadership, had their magic used against them or have been mind-controlled by those who represented illusion.

Continuity has therefore been an issue within most kingdoms. The notable exception has been the hidden kingdom of the Darklings, for even within the horse races the loss of freedom of the wild horses caused a loss of energy, hope and life force for all.

It is for this reason that the Darklings have been the custodians, not only of the cosmic life force center, but the cosmic memories. They held these even when Mother Herself lost Her memory, safeguarding those memories until they could turn them over to us. That time has come and the information that follows is from them.

Why it is necessary to know an accurate history? Firstly, to replace the lies that continue to be told to this very day about how the Fall took place and who the real perpetrators are, requires the truth be provided. Secondly, where memories are clear, accurate and strong, they become a source of power and energy.

"Know the truth and the truth shall set you free" is a proven and powerful statement because the more illusion we dispel, the higher the level of truth we can receive.

---

5 With the exception of the Pegasus and Unicorns, only four from the angel kingdoms rebelled.

Book II – Freedom from the Treadmill

Our Loop of Existence Within the Fall

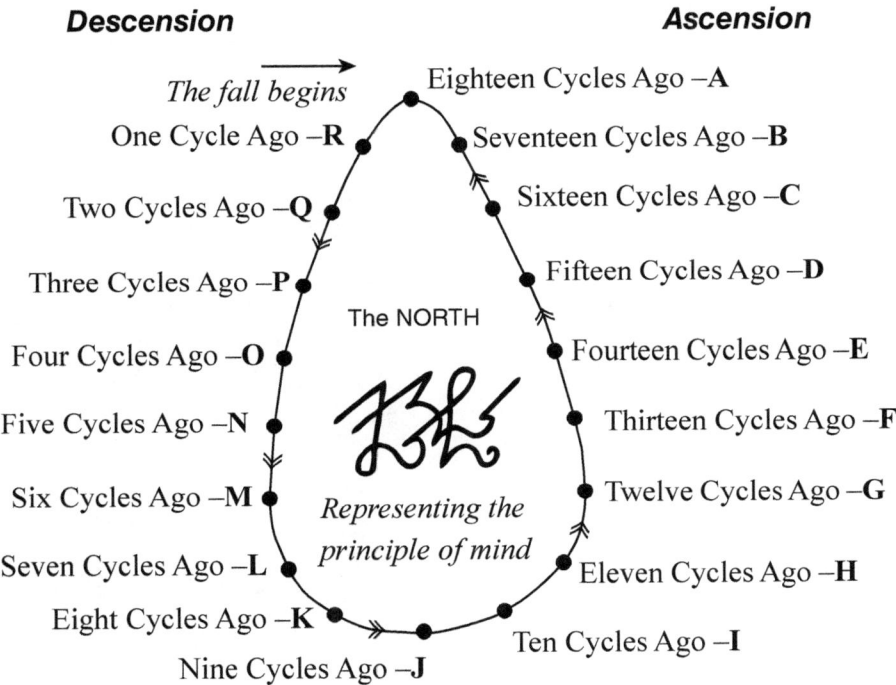

A – Britbranukheresva
B – Virshstranabirtnechparvu
C – Peleshnuastraparvet
D – Krugnavilnavek
E – Virshstaruchvi-ulesvavi
F – Michpresbarutkelechsvi-ubararut
G – Blavachseshviherestag
H – Brimineshvikluvasta
I – Stuavechkresvauvraveretek
J – Stelemirkrunesviheresta
K – Verlachbravaheshpistrana-doch
L – Silviskratnutpeleshnutvi
M – Stravukletnutheresva
N – Blishblanucherestraunet
O – Kluvarechshpi-urvavech
P – Mirvanadochstra-uvabach
Q – Kluavivachvrasteruvit
R – Elvishvraklarespi

The nine descension cycles were called:
Klubatruaneshprispretvauklesbi

The nine ascension cycles were called:
Hurplesplek-urnavestresh-abruhelesvi-kluavachvra-kreunit

Figure 11

The Eighteen Cycles
of Existence

Eighteen Cycles Ago
Britbranukheresva

Before we can know of the cycles of the Fall
We must speak of why it happened at all
Forty and four[6] cycles or levels above
An aspect of Mother reigned with love

From Her was created a God of Light
But to create him She gave Her third eye sight
She made Herself incomplete to create him that day
Thinking She would raise him closer to Her that way

But incompleteness cannot completeness create
She did not know this till it was too late
Her love for him was strong and pure
She could not see his treacheries for what they were

We turn now our tale to twenty levels above
Where a lower aspect of the one Mother loved
With one of Her lower aspects children did sire
But six children there were with evil desires

Because of the blindness we even then fell
But now it's time of the Great Fall to tell
The ones who caused eighteen cycles of life
With suffering for all and toil and strife

It was to their gain for the Fall to be
For the lower life fell, the less She could see
The more control they then could gain
The more they could torment and cause Her pain

---

6 As of April 13, 2007.

Finally captured and at their feet
The Mother no longer order could keep
A big bang happened and a fallen state
But now we tell of Earth's sad fate

By twelve star systems before surrounded was she
But now with tremendous speed they shot free
The Earth herself shot from her space
But a collision shattered her face

Once known as Tiamat, her size three times more
Now she was shattered with debris from before
Where she collided was far from here
With a planet then known as Migatuburiet

Few beings survived – humans weren't yet formed
All were in shock, losing memories from before
From Mother's hand on the planet She loved
Came human souls from realms above

Bodies She made for those that did come
To support the Mother was the motive for some
But others wanted in power to grow
For no one knew how far the decension would go

To stabilize the Earth by debris surrounded
Lord Horlet was called to help keep her grounded
As planetary lord impeccable he's been
Loving the Mother through ages unseen

Another star system then was Earth's heavenly home
Mother loved her though she seemed insignificant to some
Mother loved Earth's heart of purity
And at this time decided her destiny

On the Earth, Mother's palaces did stand
One above the ocean and one on land
The one above the ocean when She wanted to be alone
The one on land was a more public home

The landmasses then were joined into one
Their movement apart had not yet begun

We must now tell of a chosen one
How a boy[7] was chosen though very young
To represent the cycles from eighteen 'till eight
Much suffering and pain would be his fate

And now we speak of the Earth's former home
Where she was despised, loved by Mother alone
There were those who deliberately made her seem bad
This lowered Earth's frequency as it made her sad

Two mighty planets ruled by kings
Kolob[8] and Melaganiga and other planets in rings
The ruler's race by humans called Lords of All
But it was their arrogance that caused the next Fall

Shot from their midst, the Earth was repelled
And with her exile all life fell
Her surface though marred had sustained humanity
But none did survive the catastrophe

On the surface, but spirits continued to be
In the hollow Earth giants and some of humanity[9]
Much terror there was and no memory
Of anything before, and no history

---

7 He has incarnated as a young Native American boy, 6 years old in 2007.
8 Called by the Maya 'Hubnab Ku', giver of movement and measure.
9 Some 12-ft humans survived.

The fate of the landmass too appeared grim
For instability began around the rim
Those that survived because of their fear
Could no longer feel the Mother near

It was fed by those who could plainly see
That one day the Earth would a deciding force be
Deliberately they did the planet malign
That none would want her, so they could in time

These were the four gods by Mother's deceitful love sired
Who with their father's help, against Her conspired
The two evil goddesses did not yet have their power
She welcomed all six; them with love did She shower

And thus trusted they came on Earth to live
To scheme and receive from Her gifts She did give
The more there was fear, the more pushed away
The Earth was thrust on her lonely way

But some there were who were tired of fear
And once again to the Mother drew near
As they once more Mother's love could feel
They slowly changed to ascended beings

More than half ascended to a higher home
Having used adversity as a stepping stone
No longer on Earth through a sun they did move[10]
Their higher frequency the Earth did lose

---

10 They ascended as waves of civilizations have always done, through the sun of whatever star system the earth was passing through at the time. Between one-half and three-fourths ascended.

Thus the Earth did plummet into a Fall
Taking with her creations one and all
So ended the cycle eighteen ago
As all burst through the membrane into below

Scriptures That Refer to Two Great Planets Where Earth Used to Reside

Many scriptures refer to the two great planets where the Earth once resided, Kolob and Melaganiga (called Oliblish by the Egyptians). In gathering information regarding this early history of the Earth, some prophets (both modern and olden day) used the Urim and Thummim.

Explanation of the Urim and Thummim

The Urim and Thummim were delivered to Joseph Smith, Founder of the Mormon religion and its first Prophet, to enable him to translate. They were also used by Abraham to see the planet Kolob. Also called seer's stones, there are several references to the Urim and Thummim used by priests of Israel and prophets in the first five books of the Bible and also in Mormon scriptures. The priests from the tribe of Levi wore these seer's stones in breastplates.

Mormon Doctrine and Covenants: 10:1

"Now behold I say unto you, that because you delivered up those writings which you had power given unto you to translate by the means of the Urim and Thummim, into the hands of a wicked man, you have lost them ..."

Some of these seer's stone devices are still secreted in various sacred sites of the Earth. Among those sites are the hall of records in Ayers Rock, Australia; the hill of Palmyra near Manchester in Ontario County, New York and there are some in Peru, as well as others.

The Scriptures (taken from the Book of Abraham in the Mormon scripture called The Pearl of Great Price, translated from Egyptian scrolls by Joseph Smith.) Chapter 3: 1–4.

1. "And I, Abraham, had the Urim and Thummim, which the Lord my God had given unto me, in Ur of the Chaldees."

2. "And I saw the stars, that they were very great, and that one of them was nearest unto the throne of God; and there were many great ones that were near unto it."

3. "And the Lord said unto me: These are the governing ones; and the name of the great one is Kolob, because it is near unto me, for I am the Lord thy God: I have set this one to govern all those which belong to the same order as that upon which thou standest."

4. "And the Lord said unto me, by the Urim and Thummim, that Kolob was after the manner of the Lord, according to its times and seasons in the revolutions thereof; that one revolution was a day unto the Lord, after his manner of reckoning, it being one thousand years according to the time appointed unto that whereon thou standest …"

A Facsimile from the Book of Abraham

Partially translated by the prophet Joseph Smith from an Egyptian papyrus, it became part of the Mormon scripture known as The Pearl of Great Price.

Figure 12

Unlocking the Mysteries of the Hieroglyphics

Oliblish (Melaganiga) represented the feminine/receptive aspect, Kolob the masculine/proactive aspect. Energy pulsed between them. Oliblish received input directly from the Mother Goddess.

Figure 13

Explanation

*By the Mormon Prophet, Joseph Smith
With Additional Translation by Almine
(Figure 13, Unlocking the Mysteries of the Hieroglyphics)*

The Egyptian Papyrus

The prophet Joseph Smith purchased an Egyptian papyrus scroll, which is partially shown in Figure 11. The portions he was permitted to translate tell of the star system of Kolob where the Earth originated.

At the time, he was not permitted to translate portions of the hieroglyphics shown. I was permitted to translate five more portions but was also told the rest is for a later time.

1 – Kolob, signifying the first creation, nearest to the celestial, or the residence of God. First in government, the last pertaining to the measurement of time… One day in Kolob is equal to a thousand years according to the measurement of this Earth, which is called by the Egyptians Jah-oh-eh.

2 – Stands Next to Kolob, called by the Egyptians Oliblish, which is the next grand governing creation …, holding the key of power also pertaining to other planets…

3 – Is made to represent God, sitting upon His throne, clothed with power and authority; with a crown of eternal light upon his head …

4 – Answers to the Hebrew word 'Raukeeyang', signifying expanse, or the firmament of the heavens; also a numerical figure, in Egyptian signifying one thousand; answering to the measuring of time of Oliblish, which is equal with Kolob in its revolution and in its measuring of time.

5 – Is called in Egyptian Enish-go-on-dosh; this is one of the governing planets also, and is said by the Egyptians to be the Sun and to borrow its light from Kolob through the medium of Kae-e-vanrash, which is the grand Key, or in other words, the governing power, which governs fifteen other fixed planets or stars, as also Floeese or the Moon, the Earth and the Sun in their annual revolutions. This planet receives its power through the medium of Kli-flos-is-es or Hah-ko-kau-beam, the stars represented by numbers 22 and 23, receiving light from the revolutions of Kolob.

6 – Represents this Earth in its four quarters.

7 – Represents God sitting upon his throne.

8 – 21 Joseph Smith said that he was not supposed to reveal the meanings of these at that time.

Information given to Almine regarding figures not translated by Joseph Smith:

17 – The Earth had its origins here. Her name when in this star system was Ana-vi-ash-varuba.

18 – In the outer ring it clearly states that there is a higher power than the god on the throne from which all life sprang, and that the higher power is feminine.

19 – The Mother Goddess created man in her own likeness.

20 – The divine Mother is all-loving and benevolent to all life.

21 – The Mother's glory is everywhere.

Commentary on the Eighteenth Cycle

- The 18 cycles of descension comprise the Cosmos's Dream State – a time when the Feminine Aspects of the Embodiment of the Infinite entered Its dream. The very first stages of creation of individuated form required a very deep forgetfulness to forget the oneness from whence it had just come. The depth of forgetfulness of the Infinite's Embodiment makes this apparent.
- Life during these early stages of formed creation are told in a parable form. The events really did take place in the deep dream states of cosmic life, but how real is the dream?
- Six perpetrators can only exist if there are six great illusions holding them in place. Each created being represents an illusion in some way for them to be a 'separate' creation at all. It is only when we transcend a life of opposites that we become an emphasis within the unified field of existence.

The Great Illusions that Created Individuations

1. The Illusion that forms an Embodiment of the Infinite: The belief that anything can be known about the Infinite Self. Because the Self is all, nothing can be known.

2. The creation of a male counterpart, the Father, for the feminine Embodiment of the Infinite within Its dream: The belief that more than one being can exist sustains the illusion of the Father's creation as part of the dream.

3. The Six Gods and Goddesses and the Illusions that sustained them:
    - That anything can be given and done to another. This follows the illusion that more than one being can exist.

- That anything can be taught to another or known about another, since each one's reality is different and cannot be known by another.
- That an opposite pole can behave any other way than antagonistically. With opposite poles, more of one is always less of the other; or that there is anything to oppose.
- That boundaries are needed to create order. Boundaries are attempts to control life, which provokes cataclysms to then break free from the restraints of boundaries.
- The belief that anything taken can create a loss or must eventually be recompensed for. The bottom of the tube torus folds in immediately and simultaneously, even as the top folds out. For every loss there is an immediate gain, if we but look for it.
- The belief that answers, guidance or support comes from without. There is no without when we are all things; the one expressing as the many. Yet the illusion that sustains the apparent individuation of another prohibits them from gaining clear answers for the reality you are experiencing. All you need is within you to guide your life.

Seventeen Cycles Ago
Virshstranabirtnechparvu

As Earth fled from her place of birth[11]
The chosen boy lived in the Inner Earth
Representing the cycles of pain
With each Fall he suffered again

Through two star-systems her pathway led
As through this cycle of life she sped
No life on the surface could the journey survive
But on the inside diversity thrived

At times Mother left to see other stars
She wanted to see how they are
But when She left the others, it seems,
Used their chance to strengthen their schemes

During this cycle they vied for Her time
Hiding their treachery behind their smiles
Through Her love gifts were given
Their attention to Her though selfishness driven

Not many open deeds did they
As they gathered their strength for a future day
Little known were the Darklings before[12]
But now they were not known at all

---

11 Kolob was not the center of the cosmos. It was, however, earth's birthplace or origin after the big bang.
12 During the 18th cycle.

Darklings always gave Mother loyalty
She hid us, for we liked our privacy
Corruption we saw, though She could not see
We wanted to hide in the depths of the sea

Cycle eighteen and cycle seventeen still[13]
All creatures depended on Mother's good will
Uniformity throughout the cosmos prevailed
Like a child they waited for Her to save

In the footstep of dependency
Two things follow, as you shall see
Growth slows down, the first to come
Followed by feelings of rebellion

Mother did not know Her children would turn
She always gave them what they yearned
But then another cataclysm came next
Caused by the Earth who was different from the rest

Despised by others for not being the same
The Earth was rejected and put to shame
In a cosmos prizing uniformity
Something had happened only few could see

The Earth now had a wayshower become
The fate of all represented by one
Between levels of existence a membrane exists
When attempting to pass, the membrane resists

---

13 Refer to the section on 'Social Stages of Development' in *Journey to the Heart of God*.

But as the Earth traveled it was with such force
Propelled with vehemence from its original source
It tore the membrane and like a volcano
Life shot through to levels below

The Earth was blamed for the lives that were lost
That growth should come at such a cost
Was the result of resistance to change
And thus we entered the sixteenth age

Commentary on the Seventeenth Cycle

- Black magic in its broadest sense is the attempt to control life.
- The first two stages of social development, dependency and co-dependency are based on the control of the one by the many, or the one's attempt to control another. They are therefore based on black magic.
- White magic attempts to set an individual free from constraints. This mirrors the stages of independency and interdependency. In doing this, it removes a lot of the causes of pain and anger. But it still acknowledges the illusions of boundaries as something to overcome, thereby making them real.
- High White Magic sees them as unreal and thereby weakens their hold. It focuses on the indivisibility of life. It only becomes usable during later ascension cycles, yet the power to use it is then less.
- The ability to do magic increases during the descension cycles when light is less (clear perception is less). It is then that frequency is higher (a key component in doing magic).
- Tribalism in all forms, and its desire for uniformity, is very apparent during the seventeenth cycle. The reason for this is the need for great illusions to sustain form. Great illusions create great polarity.

- During great polarity, life is seen in black and white, good and bad. The message of the tribe is: You are either with us or against us. Yet if one (like the Earth) steps out of the expectations of the tribe, it leads the way for others to follow.

Sixteen Cycles Ago
Peleshnuastraparvet

The Earth all life on its surface lost
No life could live there, it was too hot
Those who from the inner Earth had come
Had all lost their lives, yes every one

The cataclysm by their own hand was done
But they all blamed Mother for what had come
The villainous gods and goddesses too
Put this tragedy to their own use

False promises made to those who were scared
"Follow us and better you'll fare"
And thus they promised what they couldn't do
Luring away many from Mother's truth

This age and the next were ones of co-dependency
With villains competing for popularity
Everyone asked "What can you do for me?"
Trying to gain Mother's trust with dishonesty

The pact of a partnership made long ago
Between a dark god and goddess now started to show
Although not embodied, for it was too hot
The dark ones gathered here to scheme and to plot

Near Arcturus Earth dwelled for a while
While Mother was absent waiting for heat to decline
More dark ones gathered on Earth to hide
Mother's absence opportunities could provide

As disharmony and darkness grew
The Earth once again was eschewed
Arcturus no longer wanted to be her home
Thus she was repelled, rejected and alone

With Earth just rejected another Fall came
All fell through the archetype's suffering and pain
And so came an end to an age of travail
And the close of a cycle once again

Commentary on the Sixteenth Cycle

- The co-dependent method of control is to give (worship, adoration, love, support) but because of what is given, there is assumed obligation of the recipient to allow him or herself to be controlled.
- In the case of dependency (tribalism), it is not much different except that the tribe's way of creating dependency is to tell you, you cannot enjoy its privileges if you do not comply, and threatens your survival by telling you that you cannot do it without them. The co-dependent does not only use false promises of external support, but shame and blame that you have no gratitude for their fake gifts and have used their 'kindness and self-sacrifice'.
- The repelling was inevitable in these two scenarios because as soon as someone grew (or started to think out of the 'box'), they became opposite light and frequency. During the ascension cycles, opposite light and frequency attract, but during the descension cycles they repel.[14]
- The tribes we attract are representative of the areas of exclusiveness (separation) that we still harbor. The co-dependent and controlling petty tyrants we attract indicate the areas of disempowerment in our lives – areas in which we seek external solutions.

14 The healing modality Belvaspata is based on this principle.

Fifteen Cycles Ago
Krugnavilnavek

But something was left in Arcturian space
Mother for them found a safe place
A group of fairies on Arcturus stayed
Where they would be safe while Mother was away

Only the ones from the surface alone
Were transplanted by Mother to an Arcturian home
None on Earth knew the fairies had left
Everyone thought from the heat they were dead

Most on Arcturus of the fairies never knew
To safeguard and keep them, She told but a few
And thus they found safety in secrecy
So Mother could visit and no one would see

Through this cycle the Earth stays hot
The Earth shoots through without a single stop
More land changes happen, volcanoes too
Did poisonous gasses into the atmosphere spew

The land and the oceans had unbearable heat
The Inner Earth had no place to retreat
There turmoil increased as water got scarce
Throughout the cycle over-population grew apace

A leader there was who order restored
Who kept the dissension from becoming a war
By Mother much loved this giant was
An impeccable leader was Egsplauvitpata[15]

---

15 See his story in *Secrets of the Hidden Realms*.

The dark goddesses finally their spirits withdrew
To escape the heat somewhere else they moved
Leaving the gods of darkness behind
To scheme to enslave all of mankind

Commentary on the Fifteenth Cycle

- The emotion of fear had arisen during the eighteenth cycle, perpetuating the myth that the tribe is needed. Anger then arose that life did not meet expectations when attempts were made to control it. Now protectiveness arose as the hostility inherent in polarity was encountered.
- Three of the artificial emotions had been created – like scar tissue they were taking the place of the lost frequencies. Protectiveness arose because of the lost sub-personality of the wise woman. Wise woman carries the knowingness that life is supportive and beneficial.
- The players in these dreams all represent something symbolically – the way that dreams do. The hiding of the fairies indicate that it was during this cycle that magical abilities on Earth were lost as well as our ability to see the Hidden Realms.
- The elves and fairies represent the child-psyche of the Earth – the Inner Babe. The interpretation of the happenings during this cycle, indicate that innocence and the love of adventure was hidden to protect it.
- This history is immensely helpful in understanding why the Inner Babe had become 'misplaced' in the center (the inner core) of the sub-personalities. It was out of the need to protect the most tender, fragile part of the psyche.
- The frequency that disappeared at this time is the knowingness that it is safe to self-explore and to express.

Fourteen Cycles Ago
Virshstaruchvi-ulesvavi

But what caused the Fall, bringing this cycle on?
Yet again the journey by the archetypal one
Propelled at a speed that few could bear
Heading for a membrane she thought would tear

But this time was different; it did not tear
She bounced off the membrane and shot through the air
It fortunate was that no collision occurred
But to a space near the central sun she returned[16]

From the speed of her movement, her atmosphere burned
But near the central sun a higher frequency returned
Restoring her climates and balance as well
She cooled off enough some heat to dispel

Mother returned to see how all fared
To strengthen the Earth and help with repair
Some from within to the surface did come
Glad to be out was everyone

Now dear to Mother one had been
Who since the great Fall[17] hadn't been seen
They called her Kalima, so she was named
For the great Fall she had been falsely blamed

---

16 All planets shot through the cosmic central sun during the big bang at the beginning of the 18th cycle.
17 Since the onset of the 18th cycle.

By Mother's side she always had stood
Supporting Mother wherever she could
Thus Mother did hide her in a pocket of space
Only now did they again see her face

Mother wanted joy for all
Hoping for peace after the Fall

But peace for Her was not to be
The six now planned great treachery
To Her was done great injuries
Causing the loss of Her memories

Throughout the cycle She stayed right here
The treacherous goddess always lingered near
Winning Her trust, gaining Her ear
Behind the smiles deceit was not clear

For a mirror was placed by Thoth in Her mind
That She could not see evil, only good could She find
The mirror the rest of the cycle remained
Allowing them all to cause Her pain

She started to miss things that were done
And began to forget She was the One
More She relied upon bad advice
Less She could see they were all lies

Kalima warned that there was deceit
She was perplexed that Mother couldn't see
She doubted herself, Mother couldn't be wrong
She did not see damage to Mother done

But Mother knew that Her discernment had fled
She doubted Herself and was by others misled
A great sadness settled upon Her heart
Ending this cycle by causing the Fall to start

The people had turned on Her, why did She not save?
Why as they expected did She not behave?
It seemed no one delivered what they said they would
So people got on as best they could

This cycle the onset of independency saw
A time when innocence was surely lost
They felt abandoned by everyone
The end of co-dependency now had begun

Commentary on the Fourteenth Cycle

- Pain, the last of the four artificial emotions, now arose due to the misperceptions of thinking that any part of the Infinite can be confined and that anything can be lost.
- The 'mirror' placed in Her mind is a matrix. It is like a kaleidoscope mirror that multiplied images of the Infinite's Embodiment. This caused multiple 'realms' or density to form as reflections around Her.
- The One started to be overwhelmed by the illusion that jointly, the many outweighed the One; especially since they all had opposite perceptions than the real Embodiment (since mirror images mirror backwards).
- The concept of aloneness and unsupportedness was born during this period. All of life seemed hostile towards that from which it sprang.

Thirteen Cycles Ago
Michpresbarutkelechsvi-ubararut

Earth to dinosaurs was a home
During this and the previous cycle did they roam
Now as this cycle had begun
A lot less heat, though close to the central sun

Now two forms of black magic came to Earth
The lesser one by Orion had been birthed
Traded to men with greed in their minds
In exchange for minerals they could mine

The minerals they used their metals to forge
They plundered the Earth their ships to engorge
The other black magic the dark god king[18]
For his own purposes to Earth did bring

Offshoots from both systems flourished here
Causing men to live in fear
Slowly a four-degree tilt took place
A danger that black magic always creates

The dark god known as Number One
Now decided into form to come
He assumed the form of one Mother loved
The God of Truth in the realms above[19]

---

18 The Number One dark god, partner to the dark goddess.
19 The god created 44 levels up.

Another one of his aspects did not take form
That the darkest part was somewhere else stored
He tried to pretend he was the God of Truth
But Mother felt this was not so

The dark goddess Her advisor was
She insisted that the God of Truth he was
Because She trusted them, She was confused
And in this way Her trust was abused

She was glad for a partner, so he married Mother
But the dark goddess in secret was his lover
Thoth and the god who was Number Two
Had formed an alliance with the other two[20]

Whenever Mother suspected deceit
They would assure Her to the contrary
Surrounded by those who did injure Her
She doubted that Her judgement was pure

They stole Her vision and told Her lies
She could not see evil with the mirror in Her mind
Warfare broke out amongst humankind
Both physical and psychic of the most terrible kind

So busy were they, they did not see
The Earth was tilting gradually
The darkness on Earth was grievous to bear
Some turned to Mother in their despair

---

20 The dark god and his dark goddess wife.

Kalima warned of something not right
She could see Mother's plight
But when the Mother Herself couldn't see
Kalima questioned her own accuracy

Kalima could not the mirror detect
Nor other things done that would Mother's judgment affect
Even the tilt of the Earth was obscured
As well as the hardship Her children endured

But now a gift unexpected did come
When one-third of the people experienced ascension
For one-third of Mother's mind then awoke
And when it did, was when Her heart broke

She tried to shield all life from Her pain
But through the cosmos it rippled again and again
All life shuddered at Her terrible grief
She tried to shield them, but did not succeed

One-third the beings could briefly see
The perpetrators' most vile treachery
How the gifts Mother gave to the goddess of lies
Had increased her power to deceive Mother's eyes

Not only did Mother her pretended sacrifices reward
But the dark god too gave her slyness rewards
In this cycle she grew in her powers and gifts
But the third who could see were made to forget

One there was with loyalty
A giant of impeccability
Egsplauvitpata ruled in the lands inside
But was prevented from coming to Her side

By the dark god aided, he was deposed
The second in line rose to the throne
Aseix ruled by treachery
Gone was the leader of integrity

Kingdoms saw the Mother's grief
A plan they made Her sadness to relieve
They decided to express more diversity
To dispel illusion and dispel the density

Not only would it Her eyes delight
But it would let them assist to turn darkness to light
The more and diverse experience
To turn illusion to light would have a better chance[21]

In the beginning some could see
But to them too the gods did injury
The treachery they saw they soon forgot
And so they forgot the traitors' plots

Mother could see a huge Fall was near
So she developed guidance clear
The Toltec Way[22] She created then
A path to walk for the world of men

This way could use adversity's force
And turn it into a power source
It would help Her remember when memories dimmed
And give Her a useful guidance system

---

21 The goal of life became to turn the unknown into the known through experience more speedily.
22 See sections on the Toltec practice in *The Ring of Truth*.

At the end of this cycle huge was the Fall
Gone were the memories of almost all
But Mother did not destroy, as they surely deserved
The villainous lives of the perpetrators

Instead She remade them pure and pristine
But their higher aspects intervened
Making sure that the plans were resumed
Their higher aspects by greed were consumed

Corrupted again their pieces that were renewed
But because She'd remade them She thought they were true
Vulnerable She was when the Fall did occur
Great was the damage then done to Her[23]

Commentary on the Thirteenth Cycle

- The tragic story of the Fall of the Embodiment of the Infinite into forgetfulness is the actual description of the One falling asleep. The great losses being described are the diminishing of light.
- But for every loss there is an immediate gain: In this case frequency gains. That this could not be seen indicates the level of dependency and the tyranny of mind and memory.
- Memory can be described as that which perpetuates the mediocrity of the past; a paltry attempt to map the unknowable boundlessness of beingness.
- What takes the place of memory is the effortless knowingness of the moment.

---

23 By the aspects of the villains that had remained in higher levels and did not Fall with their lower aspects.

- The Toltec Way[24] was a form of conduct to find our way through the mirrors and to assist in seeing behind face values.
- Because the Mother had abandoned Her own inner knowing in favor of 'external' information sources, self-abandonment had taken place. The natural result of self-abandonment is addiction. Addiction to relationship resulted.
- Even though Horlet, keeper of the Earth, and Egsplauvitpata were seen as impeccable by the skewed vision of the Mother, they later proved to be but biding their time to show their deceit. All beings in Her environment were mirror images – opposites – and were therefore antagonists when any relationship was formed. Even Kalima later became an opponent. Relationship of opposites carries its own demise.
- During this period the reflections in the mirror were mistakenly seen as creations. Nothing can be created. Everything that is real has always been – all else is but an imaginary dream.
- Because they were seen as creations, the Mother felt they had been imperfectly made and tried to fix them. This created further self-abandonment and also the belief that She could make a mistake. Fear that through failure others would suffer developed.
- The place at the center of the Tube Torus (Cosmic life) was abandoned as the Embodiment entered the mirrors, leaving only the Inner Babe at the core of life. The Embodiment of the Infinite began to pacify illusion.

---

24 It has had to change to reflect cosmic changes. See *The Way of the Toltec Nagual*.

Twelve Cycles Ago
Blavachseshviherestag

Cycles eighteen through thirteen, we fell through six small frequency bands
Now a big frequency change was at hand
Something the central sun could not stand[25]
This all occurred because the treachery had made Mother sad

So yet again we were repelled away
But Mother prevented us from being afraid
She kept a shield and hologram in place
That made us think we were still in the same space

Like a comet did we seem
Pulling behind us our debris
Some of it did burn away
As Earth searched for a place to stay

The latter part of this cycle did we come
To revolve around our present sun
Because of Earth's passage did a small moon come
Into the passage of a bigger one

Both moons from Mars thus did collide
And so formed the belt of asteroids
Part of the big moon all of the small
As well as Earth's debris the belt did form

---

25 Earth became incompatible with the central sun's high frequency.

At this time into our solar space
To Venus came the Hathor race
Twelve from Mother's palace ruled the Earth
Forming a governing council for the Earth

Mother sought stability to give
Thus formed seven lords of light here to live
Their own palace She gave to them
The council was visited much by the seven

Of the council, by dark gods persuaded
Two were corrupted, two undecided
The other eight genuinely tried
To support the Mother and spread the light

The seven lords not yet corrupted were
But already began their options to explore
The gods of darkness only when required
Did take form in order to conspire

Only the few by them targets were made
They did not yet the masses invade
They did not reveal their agendas openly
Mother was visiting here too frequently

Where Earth was during this time
Was next to Mars on the other side
A much larger planet, Nibiru by name
Into the same space with its orbit came

When they saw Earth usurping their spot
The Earth out of the way was shot
It spun her out of their way to here
The people on Earth were filled with fear

Warlike they were no matter the cost
Not once did they care that one-tenth was lost
A piece of the Earth was broken away
All that mattered was that they'd cleared the way

Mother all life together did hold
Though confidence in Her was very low
Greed now grew in Nibiruan hearts
For gold was seen as Earth broke apart

Thus ended a cycle of gloom
Further made worse by Nibiru's doom

Commentary on the Twelfth Cycle

- Protectiveness and the desire for stability stem from the desire for permanence and opposition to change – key factors in tribalism (dependency) and alliances (co-dependency).
- The seven lords represent the splitting of life into the seven directions. This is the period during which most of the cosmic creatures fell into what became the additional four directions: the vertical axis mapped out by the Kabbalah, I Ching and Tzolk'in. It is the time when the Inner Warrior, Sage, Child and Nurturer developed within each of us.
- The illusion that inner knowing should abdicate to mind and logic grew much stronger. Seven minds developed as this great fall occurred: Logical mind, right-brain non-cognitive mind (unconscious), heart-mind (sub-conscious), instinctual mind, survival mind, pro-creational mind and cellular mind.
- The battle for supremacy began to register in the body and diseases grew. The splitting of the Earth and the splitting of the brain hemispheres took place during this cycle.

Eleven Cycles Ago
Brimineshvikluvasta

Both in this cycle and the one before
Mother decided sacred treasures to store
Keeping safe creational codes
Where none can find it and none can know

Seven groups of fairies Her crown jewels kept[26]
To us She the gem of life force sent
The Unicorns and Pegasus also much had
To safely keep when times got bad

The one known as Christ from Sirius came
A small group of his followers did the same
About angels he taught that others may know
How to see angels he the people did show

Sunat Kumara on Venus did stay
Among the Hathor, he was more advanced than they
During this cycle he came and went
He wanted as much time with Mother to spend

He governed Lemuria for a thousand years
He wanted to help reduce all the tears
Climates now changed and the firmament formed
No climatic extremes, no blizzards, no storms

---

26 See photos of the fairies and the gems in *Arubafirina—The Book of Fairy Magic.*

Two layers of ice around the planet did lie
Thirty and forty thousand feet in the sky[27]
The Sun came through though no stars were seen
The entire planet became lush and green

Plants got bigger, to Mother's delight
The Earth like a garden in everyone's sight
Mother visited many more times
The size of humans now did decline

They used to be twelve feet tall
With fewer chromosomes after the Fall
Upon the surface less people were
Loss of life from Nibiru occurred[28]

At this time in Antares we find
An energy source, one of its kind
The cosmic life force, a Flower of Life sphere
Was in Antares but exploited by them there

They sold off pieces, which could create with thought
Cosmic life force was sold and bought
On Earth the same pillaging you'd find
Orion and Nibiru treaties did sign

With greedy leaders sharing the spoil
They mined and pillaged our planet's soil
They took what they wanted and then they left
Little they cared what for Earth was best

---

27 The temperature did not vary much between the poles and the equator.
28 Human life-span decreased as well.

In the smaller humans no value they saw
Pretending to be gods, they created much awe
Even the leaders believed their lies
With great technology they deceived their eyes

With the Fall, people's ability to see
Other realms and higher realities
No longer functioned, much discernment ceased
The rape of the planet this loss increased

The dark gods exploited the people's loss
They could no longer hear Mother's voice
In the inner Earth the people felt
A global catastrophe was imminent

Being wise, they hid inside
Corruption on the surface was all they could find
Catastrophe came—their predictions were right
In part caused by the loss of the people's sight

A huge eruption on the ocean floor[29]
Through the Earth's crust hot lava did pour
Tectonic plates were thrust aside
The Himalayas in a day did rise

To the dark one's glee no life survived
Except those who in inner Earth did hide
Mother's shock and grief over the loss of all
And the loss itself created the Fall
(See Fig. 14, The Cosmic Life Force Center)

---

29 The Atlantic Ocean.

Commentary on the Eleventh Cycle

- The fall in consciousness was coupled with forgetfulness and a loss of abilities. The levels of life represented by each cycle are separated by membranes. Mystics travelling between these levels of life find the membranes appearing as brittle glass-like tubes stacked on top of one another in octagonal shapes.
- The membranes are like an electric fence with the ability to steal memories. They erase the patterns of frequency (memory) from the magnetic components, as life forms move through a membrane. The membranes of cells do the same thing as they absorb the memory of the cells as to their optimal functioning and their ability to self-regenerate.
- The 'high voltage' effect causes a stroke-like effect in the brain cells. Many cells go into a 'coma' and brain capacity becomes reduced. The ability to interpret sensory data diminishes and much of life becomes out of reach and beyond our capacity to experience.
- Such a membrane exists between life and death for instance, deleting memories between incarnations. Incarnations are the microscopic representations in humans of the cosmic cycles. The membranes are electrical because they are the product of mind. Mind's addiction to controlling by knowing, causes it to divide and catagorize.

Cosmic Life Force Center
(located in the Antares System)

The cosmic life force center resembles the pattern shown above. This is known as a Flower of Life sphere. It consists of 19 perfectly interwoven circles contained in a membrane. The Flower of Life sphere holds the perfect blueprint and also all potential.

Figure 14

Ten Cycles Ago
Stuavechkresvauvraveretek

As all life fell corruption spread
Throughout the cosmos, by the dark ones fed
The cosmic chakras by other planets held
By corruption now were polluted as well

Thus Mother removed creational codes from them
And placed these in the fairy gems
As Antares the cosmic life force did sell
Mother's life force was affected as well

Thoth decided to profit, too
With some cosmic life force much he could do
He managed to get some, but hid it well[30]
Thoth had it but the seven lords could tell

In this cycle the Sphinx was built
It was here the life force was hid
Mother for the Lords a building did make[31]
They the life force to the Halls of Amenti did take

But let us tell you of Thoth's deed most vile
What he traded in order his prize to acquire
After Mother had hidden the last[32]
Her mind and memory failed very fast

---

30 In the Sphinx.
31 See reference to Halls of Amenti in *Secrets of the Hidden Realms*.
32 The last sacred object or information.

At last She no longer knew who She was
Forgotten Her identity of all that She was
Thoth sold Her secret and Her as well
To the Kings of Antares he Her secret did tell

Drain Her life force and you shall live
Her life force immortality gives
King Oxanuhuratep married his prize
And because She could not see with Her third eye
An etheric tube he placed into Her side
Draining Her life force to lengthen his life

Mother did not know of their treachery
So in the beginning happy was She
But why She felt ill She could not tell
Only on Earth did She feel really well

The goddess of lies Her stepdaughter was
For she at this time an opportunity saw
Wherever Mother went, she followed behind
Seemingly loving, pretending to be kind

Not many people on Earth's surface there were
With landmasses still shifting it was not very secure
But the stepdaughter Mother loved wanted to come
For here dwelled the dark god Number One

Unknown to Mother, the tube in her side
Was causing the loss of Her strength and Her sight
She relied on the stepdaughter to give Her advice
She did not know she was the goddess of lies

The seven lords saw Mother's strength fail
They grew concerned when they saw Her ail
But the dark god and the goddess of lies
Insisted that She was fine

Now the dark god and goddess in earnest began
The implementation of their vicious plan
The whole cosmos jointly they wanted to rule
Using Mother as their useful tool

The advice She was given played into their hands
They tricked Her to help with their devious plans
The King of Antares was tortured by them
And revealed how Mother's energy was drained and then
They, as well as Thoth did the same
Controlling Mother by causing Her pain

Warfare broke out between the lands
With weapons[33] obtained from alien hands
Lemuria, Atlantis, the Middle East too
Decided a hole in the firmament to shoot

With weapons of power in two places they shot
To drown their enemies was their plot
But the results they got went far beyond
The ice shields both collapsed at once

A global flood the result there was
Two percent of all life was lost
Mother now forgot everything
As one cycle closes a lower one begins

---

33 Weapons using zero point energy that Thoth had obtained from Antares.

The Rape of the Cosmic Life Force Center

The pillaging of the cosmic life force center played a large part in engineering the continuing descension and Fall of the cosmos. The cosmos can be said to be the Mother Goddess's larger body. In other words, in the same way we have an etheric, emotional and mental body (and others) surrounding our physical form, so the cosmos is the fields around Mother's form.

What therefore happens to Mother ripples throughout the cosmos and the reverse is true as well. Every time a piece of the cosmic life force was lost or sold, it affected Her as an individuated being as well. Also, the 'as above so below' principle applied. Because they were successfully exploiting the cosmic life force, it became easier to do it to Her without anyone noticing or intervening.

Mother had very little support and assistance. The few who tried were themselves overpowered by the higher aspects of the perpetrators. But one may well ask, "What about Mother's higher aspects? The feminine portions of Herself She kept separating out to open spaces or realms to form a place where the Fall could take place?"

There are some obvious reasons why they were not very proactive or effective in helping the positive aspect of Mother whose story we're telling.

- If the above affects the below, and the feminine, negative polarity aspect in the Grand Realms of Mother was drugged, we can expect the same here. The feminine aspects of the Mother within Creation were over-polarized into deep joy and bliss. Because the drugged goddess from above was not pulsing with Her positive aspect within the Fall, neither were the feminine aspects within the cycles of the Fall. This disturbed the dynamic balance that produces power. The positive aspect became over-polarized in activity (which caused Her to spread Herself too thin). The feminine parts of Herself left in realms above became over-polarized in inactive bliss. They were so expanded they could not see the smaller picture, like how their counterpart was being damaged. *(Figure 15, How the Fall Affected the Positive and Negative Aspects of the Mother)*

- Every feminine aspect left to hold open space was also subject to being interfered with and damaged because of two reasons: Firstly, it successfully happened 'above', thus also below. Secondly, the true source of deceit and hostility came from much, much higher[34] and was therefore more powerful than all of them.
- Part of the damage done to all pieces of the Mother in the cycles of the Fall is forgetfulness. This caused all of them to forget that the one posing as the highest goddess in the Fall is the same imposter who took over Mother's throne in the Grand Realms. They forgot that they had hidden the three top true Mothers. They therefore at times, and especially towards the end of the ascension of the cosmos, took directions from her. This hindered hugely rather than helped.
- The initial plan was that when the positive aspect of the Mother fell and the cycles of the Fall began, that the feminine aspect of the Mother who had entered the Fall would be the one who would step Her pieces down to hold space open, but She and the two Mothers below Her, were in hiding. The positive Mother therefore had to give away every conceivable feminine part remaining within Her, in order to open spaces to contain life in an orderly manner. The problem with this was that it is the feminine part within us that accesses the unknown behind the appearances, an ability She lost as She gave each piece away. Secondly, it was diluting the power and ability of the feminine pieces, as the positive Mother had less and less to leave.

---

34 It actually came from 44 levels up from Mother's first male creation, the King of Truth.

How the Fall Affected the Positive and Negative Aspects of the Mother

⊖ = Receptive unit (negative polarity)
⊕ = Proactive unit (positive polarity)

The Grand Realms
(from which the Fall began)

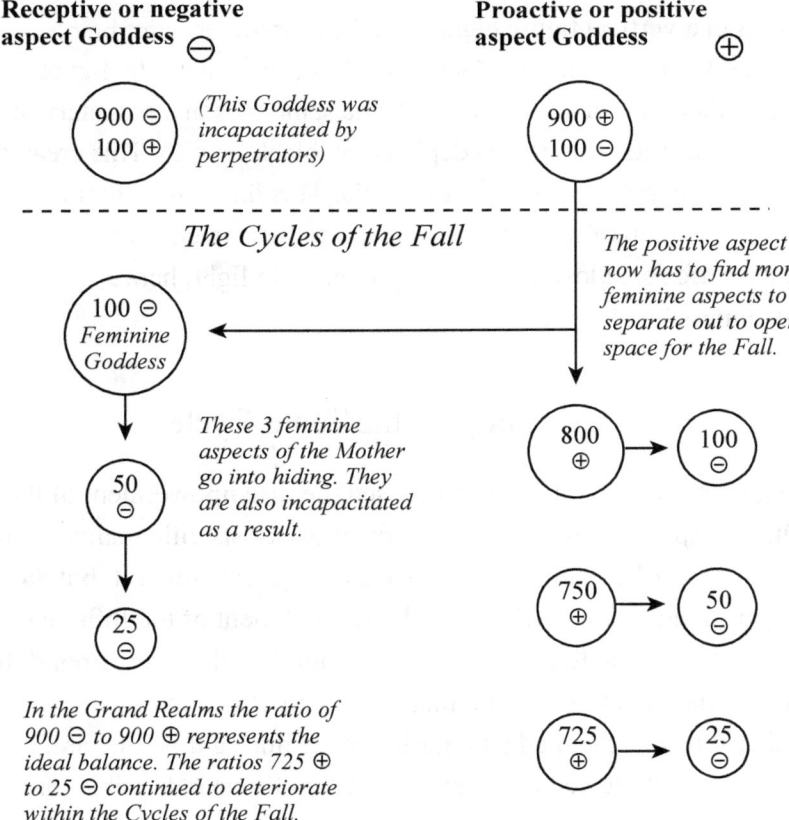

Receptive or negative aspect Goddess ⊖

900 ⊖
100 ⊕

(This Goddess was incapacitated by perpetrators)

Proactive or positive aspect Goddess ⊕

900 ⊕
100 ⊖

The Cycles of the Fall

100 ⊖
Feminine Goddess

50 ⊖

25 ⊖

These 3 feminine aspects of the Mother go into hiding. They are also incapacitated as a result.

The positive aspect now has to find more feminine aspects to separate out to open space for the Fall.

800 ⊕ → 100 ⊖

750 ⊕ → 50 ⊖

725 ⊕ → 25 ⊖

In the Grand Realms the ratio of 900 ⊖ to 900 ⊕ represents the ideal balance. The ratios 725 ⊕ to 25 ⊖ continued to deteriorate within the Cycles of the Fall.

Figure 15

The Effects of the Loss of Cosmic Life Force

- Chakras receive information from higher realms. All chakras are vitalized by the Haran chakra behind the belly button where the life force center is located. Depleting the life force center affected all other chakras where creational codes had been kept. Creation was therefore infused with less and less life force.
- In a being living in the timeless place of the Eternal Now, life force flows in a vertical figure eight with the cross-over point being behind the belly button[35]. As the life force grew less, the figure eight tilted until it was horizontal (the same reason a planetary axis would tilt if its life force is depleted by black magic). This created linear time and the principle of inertia. This flat figure eight is called the loop of time, or the Zuvuya by the ancient Maya.
- Lower life force lowers the ability to contain light, hence awareness levels drop.

Commentary on the Tenth Cycle

- The greatest dilemma that has caused the disempowerment of the One is exposed here: The environment of our specific reality is but a reflection of ourselves. For this reason, we can affect it, but the mirror image cannot affect us. The Embodiment of the Infinite can affect the cosmic life force center, but not the other way around. It is only the belief that it can, that creates an effect on us.
- Other illusions that had a major influence during this time are:
    - That anything can be given away when life is indivisible, or that anything can be stolen.

---

35 Later in the book we will see that this point, as the location of the life force center, has been moved to the heart in all beings.

- That the needs of the many are more valuable than the needs of the one when they are two opposite poles.
- War is the necessary remedy for stagnation. Yet stagnation is overlooked as the root of many atrocities. Stagnation occurs when there is too much feminine, receptive or inactive energy.
- The concept of order as beneficial and disorder as harmful is a skewed perception. That which seems like disorder from a lower perspective always becomes order when you raise perception high enough.

Nine Cycles Ago
Stelemirkrunesviheresta

From the shock of the flood caused by Thoth
Felt by Mother and the people both
Consciousness yet again regressed
The feminine was increasingly suppressed[36]

Spiritual darkness came yet again
As the flood receded from the land
Completely separated now the landmasses were
Some said the salt in the water came from Mother's tears

As She was suppressed, all women were too
Male supremacy was taught to the youth
The dark ones took a great delight
In humiliating Mother in Her tragic plight

Out of the great palace She now was
The dark god lived there with the goddess of lies
Thoth and Number Two lived there, too
The dark goddess lived in Mother's rooms

Some races now others enslaved
Mirroring that which with Mother was the same
Thoth now splits himself into good and bad
The good one wanted Mother's love to have

---

36 In cycles 10, 9 and 8 ago.

The bad one plots to take what he can
To take whatever Mother has
Depths of despair were reached at this time
As morals and virtue continued their decline

Black magic abounded as bands of Toltecs withdrew
Secret places shielding their mystery schools
In what is China, Peru and the Caucases too
In the Rocky Mountains they hid, darkness to eschew

That which they foresaw did surely come
A massive catastrophe killing almost everyone
The axis did tilt, the Earth did flood
The dark ones pretended to help and be good

The Pacific[37] north did rush over shores
The tidal waves carrying man and mammoths before
The Atlantic with ice southward sped
Debris by Fallen cities fed

Even the Lords of Amenti who still tried to do right
Thought the gods of darkness were gods of light
Mother couldn't protect the people any more
Thus this cycle ended just like before

Commentary on the Ninth Cycle

- The tube torus of existence needs to be examined in order to understand how these cataclysmic events are able to occur.
- The tube torus accumulated the debris of unresolved issues and their unyielded insights around the outer edge – the gap between the breaths. This was encountered over and over again as the

---

37 The Pacific Ocean. Some Aleutian islands were formed by mammoth bones.

consciousness of Earth and its inhabitants went around the moving revolutions of the tube torus.
- But the opposite was over-looked as an additional cause of increased opposition. There was not only debris building up as the out-breath turned into the in-breath (on the rim), but also as the in-breath turned into the out-breath (in the middle of the tube torus). As an out-breath and in-breath completed itself, it breathed its last into this inner circle. It therefore held the old, toxic patterns of the eons of in- and out-breath cycles of life – one of the primary reasons why purification and re-creation attempts by the Embodiment of the Mother failed. Life would just become contaminated again.

Eight Cycles Ago
Verlachbravaheshpistrana-doch

All of a sudden a new sound was heard
A new language of Mother[38] – it was the third
One before the Fall there was, another
Was spoken after the Fall by the Mother

Now a new language She spoke, the dark ones were vexed
By this sudden change, they were very perplexed
But the tones of the cosmos were restored by Her tongue
Bringing some healing to everyone

The change created a small ascent
It was slow enough that they could not detect
But control they wanted whatever the cost
Through Her changing Her speech, they felt control had been lost

The dark gods enforced their own form of speech
On any realms their influence could reach
Their language caused the masculine to dominate
Gave supremacy to the surface mind that now separates

Women were turned into a man's property
A status symbol of a man's prosperity
Though Mother managed to bring a little light
Wars still raged as neighbor against neighbor did fight

---

[38] See Part VI of Book III in later part of this book for more information on "Languages of the Mother".

But a small ray of light penetrated Her mind before long
Just enough for Her to know that something was wrong
A falseness She felt in the smiles that were there
But she was confused, the feeling was everywhere

Those that were true from Her were kept away
Spies around Her were commanded to stay
They watched all She did, both night and day
Under the dark one's control She remained this way

The populace had stopped relying on others
They could no longer hear the voice of the Mother
They each started to trust only themselves
Confidence in leaders drastically fell

And so co-dependence to independence did yield
Each wanted gain to get or to steal
But in small pockets where commerce thrived
Instead of independence, interdependence survived

As cooperation caused the flow of trade
Others noticed that an increased profit made
When enough lived this way, the frequency raised
First the Earth, then the cosmos, the jump to a higher level made

Commentary on the Eighth Cycle

- It was during this cycle that the Inner Feminine Nurturer awoke and started to speak. A feminine, more vowel-based language ensued. The reason that this awakening took place is that the stage of interdependence had been reached – the last stage on the movement away from the tube torus's center before the cosmic journey turns inward on its journey towards the center. The masculine is thwarted at this juncture, from further linear expansion and dominance. It has to slow down as it encounters the edge.
- This outward journey can be called an ascension of light (masculine) and the inward journey, an ascension of frequency (feminine). The outward journey is the time during which the Inner Warrior and its opposite, the Inner Nurturer are dominant – it is the vertical axis of expression. The Inner Child and Inner Sage are the dominant forms of expression when life moves inward – the horizontal axis of existence.

Seven Cycles Ago
Silviskratnutpeleshnutvi

In this cycle Mother more self-knowledge gained
She watched and listened and learnt from Her pain
Though yet not aware of who She is in reality
Something whispered "This is not your true identity"

Her feminine aspect though hidden from view
From the top of the cycles yet whispered to Her truths
It filtered down from the very top
"Know in your heart, a servant you are not"

She noticed that others that also served
Were treated in many ways different from Her
Still to kings She prostituted was
Her humiliation was more than anyone else's was

To escape She wanted and so She planned
Observing their schemes and wicked plans
They were occupied with something they'd seen
The cosmic ascension, which previously unnoticed had been

They hoped that by producing enough fear
That a cosmic descension soon would be near
Volcanoes and earthquakes with technology produced
To frighten the people, were tools that they used

On Earth a kingdom of dragons did live
No respect to Mother[39] did they give
An agreement with the dark gods did they make
When the six ruled the cosmos, the rule on Earth dragons would take

So they helped to harm the Mother of all life
That they could rule when the time was right
From men to hide, dragons maintained a shield
The dark ones felt that without it, more terror would there be

The shield was removed, the dragons fumed
By arrogant rage their leader consumed
War there was with most planets involved
Between Atlantis and Lemuria a trade dispute unresolved

During this cycle Thoth plotted and schemed
Of ruling the Earth he planned and dreamed
The darkest powermongers found among men
Formed an alliance in a distant land then[40]

With weapons of power from star-brothers obtained[41]
They hoped over Atlantis and Lemuria advantage to gain
Over those two continents advantage they had
Though much smaller, they had the upper hand

The two large powers now united were
The small group must be stopped, of that they were sure
With technology most fearsome by them employed
All in that country were destroyed

---

39 Described in "The Old Dragon Insults Mother", *Journey to the Heart of God*.
40 What is today known as Patagonia, located at the tip of South America.
41 The Pleiadeans.

But now that the darkest of men were gone
The frequency raised, benefiting everyone
This cycle closed, to the dark ones' ire
As the Earth[42], then the cosmos both rose higher

Commentary on the Seventh Cycle

- The ability for sub-personalities to interdependently work together and be able to communicate with one another is crucial to acquiring self-knowledge. The necessity for a common form of language between the sub-personalities is a key component of successful cooperation.
- The common 'language' between the sub-personalities of the vertical and horizontal axes (the two sides of the tube torus), is found in the poetic images of the Poetry of Dreaming and the Poetry of Awakening.

---

42 Because the earth is an archetype, her rise in frequency affected all of the cosmos.

The Poetry of Dreaming and the Poetry of Awakening

The Poetry of Awakening is the key to communication between the nurturer and the impeccable spiritual warrior. It is a series of poetically descriptive sentences that convey the layers of feeling behind the description and give it its ambient qualities.

The Poetry of Awakening serves as the communication device of the vertical axis of existence. The Inner Nurturer and Inner Warrior are the components of this axis, which can be described as the mind-based approach to life. The mind has a left-brain (conscious) and a right brain (unconscious) way of accessing and communicating information.

This poetic method is used by the unconscious whereas the Poetry of Dreaming is used by the sub-conscious or heart-mind. It enables communication between the Inner Child and Inner Elder of the horizontal axis.

Shrivat Satva Yoga uses the Poetry of Dreaming to help clear past Dream Cycles or Descension Cycles of life and the times when debris of unresolved issues gather in the sub-conscious. The Poetry of Awakening is used in the Saradesi Satva Yoga to help clear the accumulated debris of Ascension Cycles that gather in the unconscious parts of the mind.

Example of the Poetry of Dreaming
'Purple currents fold like glittering ribbons through endless oceans of sunlit blue. I carry the sky within my breast.'

Example of the Poetry of Awakening
'With a thunderous roar, lightening cracks the black egg of the night. In the valley below, on a cottage windowsill, a candle flame wavers but folds back the darkness of the night. Wrapped in her shawl, a child sleeps in his mother's arms.'

Communication Between the Sub-personalities
Clearing Debris from Past Incarnations

Excerpt from *The Scroll of Namud*

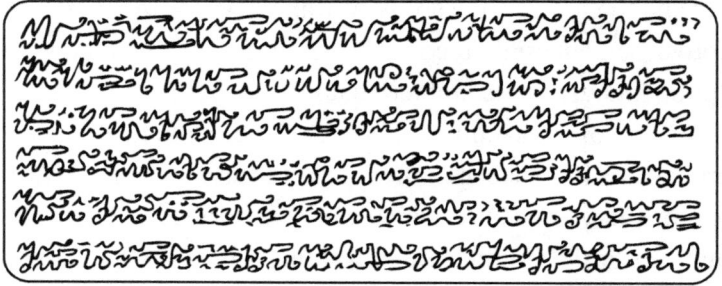

Figure 16

The Poetry of Dreaming is beneficial at all times for the resolving of deep psychic trauma from past cycles of incarnation. It is a key component of Shrihat Satva Yoga, which serves the same purpose of releasing the debris from past lives.

Translation of the Scroll of Namud

From the Motherland[43] we call Shalmali, great wisdom was spread to the many peoples of the Earth. Wise masters called Nagas[44], which means 'gates of wisdom', were sent to teach. They took tablets of wisdom with them and separated into groups of two, copying these tablets so that they could share them with different people.

---

43 Lemuria
44 Called Naguals or Nacaals in some tongues.

They taught the Naga language to all in walled temples called 'Chaldi'[45] or 'Kaldi', meaning 'walls'. Seven sets of holy records were taken through high mountains (Himalayas) to the land of Monassa (India) and placed in Kaldi temples in seven cities. The records were kept by divinely inspired poets or sages called 'Rishis'. These seven cities became known as Rishi cities.

The records taught yoga, which means 'gates of the body' to the people. The greatest of these was Devi Satva Yoga.

Devi Satva Yoga was designed to create enlightenment by opening various sets of gates in the human body. It consisted of Irash Satva Yoga, Shrihat Satva Yoga and Saradesi Satva Yoga[46], the latter being the yoga of the Fountain of Youth.

> *Minikva ares prihat uruva hachte.*
> Within man are the answers to the starry skies.

---

45 Where the Biblical nation, the Chaldeans, get their name.
46 See www.yogaofillumination.com.

The Seer Almine Receives a Scroll of Ancient Records

Almine has been photographed in various locations as she receives scrolls, which she later translates and shares with her students. The scrolls, which appear on her head, are seen in this interdimensional photo taken at a retreat in Sedona, Arizona, 2010.

Figure 17

Records translated by Almine, photographed interdimensionally

Two photographs taken by B. Rotzoll.
These records were translated months before the photos were taken.

Figure 18

Note: For many years Almine has translated tablets and records from inter-dimensional sources that reveal sacred information previously unavailable to humanity. In the last months of 2009, some of her students were able to obtain photographic evidence that these materials exist. See the preceding page for examples of inter-dimensional photos of tablets previously translated by Almine.

Drawing of the Scroll Translated by Almine

Tablets drawn and translated by Almine months before they were photographed.

Figure 19

Clearing Past Incarnational Cycles

Excerpt from *Labyrinth of the Moon*

Cosmic cycles of life fall into two categories: those that can be called the ascension cycles and those that are called the descension cycles.

There are 12 electrical, masculine, light-based cycles; these are the ascension cycles. Likewise there are 12 cycles of a feminine, magnetic, frequency-based nature. Each of these has been repeated many times by all creatures as incarnation cycles.

The unresolved issues of those cycles, such as old belief systems, memories of pain and other distorted emotions are presented for resolution in dreams. There are 24 depths of dreaming, with the 12 more shallow ones communicating to us through dream symbols. The 12 deepest dream states are the feminine, non-cognitive states that cannot be interpreted through dream symbols and produce what to us seems like a deep, dreamless sleep. They speak to us through art and the Poetry of Dreaming.

This unique poetry communicates through omissions – that which is not said – imparting multiple depths of meaning revealing themselves as feelings and qualities. Although the Poetry of Dreaming uses literary devices such as assonance, alliteration, personification and sustained epithets, their use has profound purpose that transcends the obvious. The same applies to the use of adjectives.

Its concise but powerful descriptive quality is reminiscent of the poetic form of Haiku, but whereas Haiku is bound by a rigid structure, the Poetry of Dreaming is not. Haiku provides the essence of simplicity that lies within the complexity of appearances. The Poetry of Dreaming whispers through its rich imagery of the primordial origins of the moment.

Upon reaching a high level of enlightenment, the master becomes an androgynous being. Having lost all other identities, he or she now loses the identity of gender. This is done by balancing the proactive and receptive qualities within. Resolving the 12 feminine and 12 masculine incarnation cycles brings this desired state to fruition.

The Poetry of Dreaming is used to open non-cognitive communication with the deeper states of dreaming. This allows the issues of very old cycles of life to come to the surface for cancellation by the sound elixirs used during yoga, or while sleeping or meditating. Read one before meditating or at bedtime. Soon you may find yourself waking up with one of your own. Do not try and interpret the image cognitively; absorb it like a sponge, becoming one with it. You will find yourself altered in a positive way without knowing how it occurred.

Further Examples of the Poetry of Dreaming

Purple currents fold like glittering ribbons through endless oceans of sunlit blue. I carry the sky within my breast.
***
*The dolphin jumps through the hoop of the moon.
Rings ripple through the stars.*
***
*The mountains snake across the plains
like a lazy python in the sun.*
***
*Wild geese, like a clanging chain, pull the moon
from the web of the willow tree.*
***
*Lured by the softness if its feathered nest,
the mighty eagle rests.*

Further Examples of the Poetry of Awakening

The laughter of children tumbling across the meadow grass is answered by the steady creaking of the old mill. In the distance a barking pup runs to join in the fray. Disturbed from his slumber by the merriment, the owl in the rafters turns his back on the noise. The whispering river carries the moment downstream to share with the willow trees.

***

A blushing swan in the sun's last rays, sailing down a gilded path. A blossom newly fallen from the cherry tree bobs up and down on the waves of his wake. One by one, the frogs start their evening serenade. The evening star peeks over the edge of the night.

Six Cycles Ago
Stravukletnutheresva

Softly was whispered into Mother's ear
A secret suggestion for Her to hear
From the top of the realms Her female aspect spoke
"Cast off your burdens, Cast off your yoke

Your dream body trapped in your body has been
In the dreamtime let it roam free
Then much can be accomplished while you sleep
The dream body no one a prisoner can keep"

Mother now during Her dream state
Then thousands of demons did create
To embody the chaos and keep it from men
She made an underworld prison for them

Lucifer and nine thousand nine hundred and nine
Were meant to be in their prison confined
But the number one dark god has a different plan
He wants to free them if he can

A hologram he made of a very large beast
A creature called Afxghelm he pretended to be
He summoned them forth with sacrifices of blood
To do his bidding, fear they did spread

With Lucifer's embodiment, a scapegoat was he
The dark ones blamed him for their foul deeds
But the demons existence brought light to men
For now they knew they were not like them

Those who were light now more appreciated were
Though they did not know Mother, they'd forgotten her
It seemed there were rewards for being good
If the lesson of Patagonia was properly understood

Mother tried the palace to escape
Amongst the masses to make Her way
Destitute was She, completely alone
No way to survive and without a home

She could not make it and so She came back
At least in the palace there was no lack
The dark ones felt increasing alarm
Things turned out good, when they had meant them to harm

Mother's dream body upon them could spy
They had to find another place to hide
On the dark side of the moon, plotting they tried
But consciousness rose like an incoming tide

All their scheming to naught did come
As this cycle raised to another one

Commentary on the Sixth Cycle

- The cosmos was, during this cycle, on an inward journey of frequency ascension. All poles flourish at the expense of their opposite poles. When frequency grows, light fades; the reason memories fade as well.
- The twelve pure pairs of emotion[47] became more dominant, bringing more feeling based insight and guidance in everyone's lives.

---

47 See page 182 for instructions on how to "Integrate the 12 Pair of Pure Emotions".

The Pure Pairs of Emotions

Positive Aspect	Negative Aspect
1. **Love** – the desire to include	**Trust** – the desire to surrender (replaces fear)
2. **Inspiration** – the desire to be inspired and to inspire (replaces anger)	**Peace** – the desire to be at ease (replaces protectiveness)
3. **Creativity** – the desire to create	**Pleasure** – the desire to be delighted
4. **Empathy** – the desire to connect	**Acknowledgement** – the desire to see the perfection
5. **Generosity** – the desire to give	**Receptivity** – the desire to receive
6. **Encouragement** – the desire to encourage or be encouraged	**Beauty** – the desire to be uplifted
7. **Communication** – the desire to express	**Assimilation** – the desire to integrate
8. **Passion** – the desire to know	**Joy** – the desire to live
9. **Achievement** – the desire to excel	**Fun** – the desire to revel
10. **Enlightenment** – the desire to enhance or be enhanced (replaces pain)	**Contentment** – the desire to retain
11. **Empowerment** – the desire to be of service	**Humor** – the desire to be amused
12. **Growth** – the desire to expand	**Satisfaction** – the desire to be fulfilled

The Twelve Pairs of Pure Emotions

1. **Trust and Love** – These are the core emotions for the new creation of existence and replace fear. As old programming of fear breaks down in every being, the new reality of trust reveals itself. All else is just an illusion.

2. **Peace and Inspiration** – These form the second ring, the desire to be at home, to feel totally at ease. These rings build on each other; we cannot feel peace when trust is not present. These attitudes come when we cease to strive and are fully at ease within the moment.

3. **Creativity and Pleasure** – The link between Creativity and Pleasure is apparent, as the more pleasure fills our life, the more the muse stirs us into creativity. The more creative we become, the more our pleasure increases. This pair of emotions, together with that of trust and peace, forms the core of the new creation.

4. **Acknowledgement and Empathy** – We must see the ever-unfolding perfection underlying appearances. It isn't enough to acknowledge that the perfection is there, then feel victimized later. Do we not realize that we have co-created whatever is in our life? If we focus on that which we love, new creation will flow. If we focus on that which we don't like, the change won't come. In this new creation, therefore, we have come into our spiritual maturity; we have become co-creators with the Infinite.

5. **Receptivity and Generosity** – There is a law of compensation decreeing that imbalance in any part of existence must have an equal and opposite movement to correct it. There is just one requirement, however, and that is receptivity. When we give, we

must not think that such generosity depletes us. Rather let us see how generosity and receptivity form one long continuous flow.

6. **Beauty and Encouragement** – Beauty is just a glimpse into the perfection of the indwelling life behind form. Every time we recognize beauty, we are encouraged (encouragement being its opposite pole).

7. **Assimilation and Communication** – Too little true assimilation of information (which is accessed light) takes place in the world for several reasons. The assimilation of other's communications enriches us. Their diversity can carve new facets in our own life; new perspectives that leave us enhanced. When we feel truly heard, the desire to communicate (its opposite aspect) becomes more active as well.

8. **Passion and Joy** – When social conditioning has left the impression that it is unsafe to fully participate in the game of life, we may hang back in the safety of the known, afraid to make ourselves a target by being noticed. If we deny our desire to express passionately long enough, we end up being strangers to passion. As passion explores the multitude of possibilities through which we can express, so joy is concentrated on the simplicity of the moment. Joy is a mindset, a certain focus that sees the perfection of the here and now, recognized by the deep feeling of satisfaction it brings.

9. **Fun and Achievement** – We've possibly all heard the saying that someone we know 'works hard and plays hard'. That's because the two go hand in hand. Fun without achievement is a shallow, unfulfilling life. Achievement without the fun that brings quality to the journey leads to an equally unsatisfying life.

10. **Contentment and Enlightenment** – Contentment knows that it is living perfect moments. The desire to enhance and enlighten the life of another is the sincere wish that insight will change despair into contentment for another as well.

11. **Empowerment and Humor** – Empowerment is the desire to serve. Humor laughs at life, laughs at self and, instead of blaming, laughs at the folly of others. It cannot take anything too seriously because it knows without a shadow of doubt that we're just engaged in a play. It helps by empowering the beggar, not because he seems needy, but just because it is his role. The play must go on because it has value.

12. **Growth and Satisfaction** – The way growth now takes place is new. It used to be the result of delving (painfully, at times) into the unknown, eventually turning it into the known through experience. Growth now comes through support. How will we know when we've found it? The deep satisfaction of our hearts will tell us we've just lived our highest truth.

The Twelve Pure Pairs of Emotions

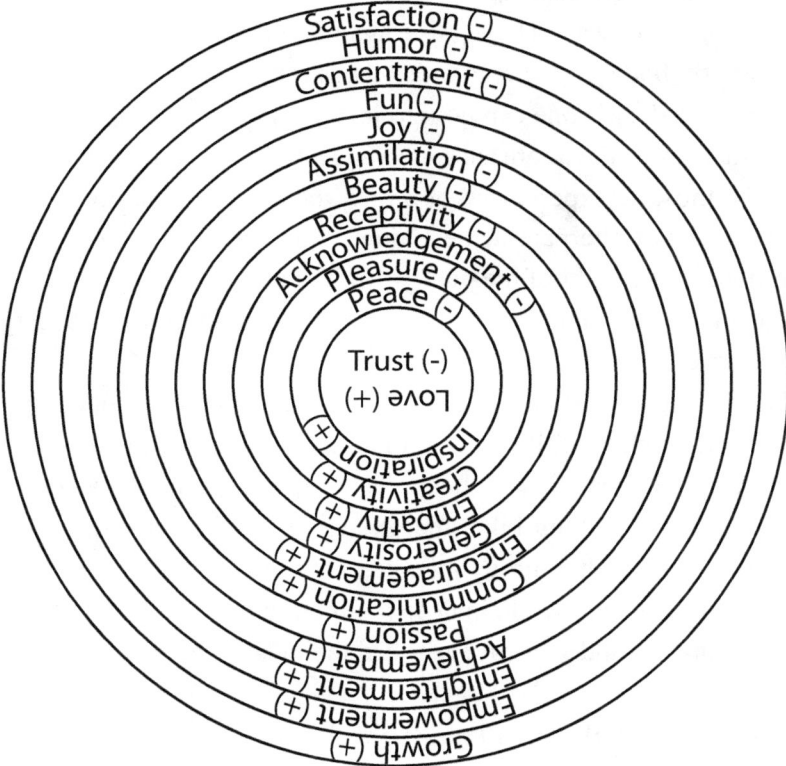

Each band represents a paired set of emotions.

Figure 20

Integrating the Emotions

Each pair of emotions represents a ring containing both its masculine and feminine aspects. They pulse against each other to enhance the qualities of both. In other words, the stronger one feels a specific emotion, the deeper one can go into its opposite aspect.

Furthermore, the more strongly an emotion is felt, the more its opposite must be experienced or an overbalance results. For instance, if one does not alternate achievement with fun, it can become blind ambition, losing sight of the quality of the journey.

To internalize an emotion, we approach it from the largest perspective:

- While in a meditative state, visualize your heart center opening wider and wider until you can imagine seeing the whole Earth in it.
- Imagine and visualize the heart center opening at a rate beyond the speed of light until the solar system, the galaxy and then many galaxies are visible through the heart.
- Continue opening while in deep meditation until the whole cosmos is within you and you have reached the membrane that contains it all.
- The large central sun will now be within you and you will see its arms of light spiraling outwards, consisting of trillions upon trillions of galaxies like specks of light.
- Remind yourself that you are a consciousness superimposed over all that is and all that you see.
- From this large perspective, feel the frequency of the emotion ripple through you as you envision all that evokes it.
- Sustain it until it is strong, potent and all you can feel.
- When you've become the emotion, understand and observe how it pulses with its opposite aspect.

- When you can feel them both, move on to the next emotion while keeping the expanded awareness.
- Each pair of emotions should be explored and experienced for about half an hour.

Five Cycles Ago
Blishblanucherestraunet

During this cycle Thoth implements his plan
To gain popularity and influence man
With science from other planets gleaned,
Tricks and magic, divine he seemed

Benign and benevolent he made himself seem
None could see how evil he'd been
The other dark gods were not fooled
They knew he wanted the planet to rule

Atlantis, always Thoth's stronghold had been
His kingdom to destroy, number one schemed
Formidable weapons they created in that land
A seeming accident was what number one planned

Though no one ever knew the part he played
The dark god a massive explosion did create
Like a volcano the Earth spewed forth
Two-thirds of Atlantis in minutes was destroyed

Whenever many souls to the spirit world leave
Those that remain behind have strengthened beliefs
Since the outer world as reliable had failed the test
Many embarked on a spiritual quest

The frequency therefore rose again
But that was not all that this cycle did change
Mother finally left one day,
Through the planning of her dream body taken away

Through planning and magic Her body left too
To a place in deep space on a solitary moon
A loop of time She did create
She prolonged Her ability to rest that way

While she rested, her burdens much eased
The effect on the cosmos was one of peace
She studied the villains and how they behaved
This She did while staying away

The cosmos suffered when Mother was in pain
Now, with Her at peace, it rose again

The Story of King Neptune and The Real Afxghelm

King Neptune is a being of the God-Kingdom who, when he takes form, is slightly more than six feet tall. When not in form, he appears as a blue light. He is one of nine kings of Neptune but for the last five million years has been trapped here on Earth. It occurred as follows:

Three of his friends, known only by the letters R, X and Y, persuaded him to visit the Earth five million years ago. He left a hologram of himself behind and came with them. I have had to use a hologram when I have been sent on a spiritual assignment at a time when I have a class to teach. The hologram is tangible and has the knowledge I would have. No one can tell the difference. The result of this is that, in King Neptune's case, no one knew he had left and he hasn't yet been missed.

The group traveled without a space ship, teleporting through a time/space portal between Earth and Neptune. There is only one of these portals on Earth, located within the Grand Canyon. While they were here, the portal was accidentally destroyed by what seemed to be a huge monster about the length of five or six Titanic ships. Thus they were trapped by the monster called Afxghelm.

They do not have a palace under the water. Instead, the whole ocean is their home. The primary function of King Neptune and his friends is the production and balancing of minerals in the world's oceans.

During the Earth's ascension, which most are entirely unaware of[48], the Earth moved through the Sun and what is called the realms of Arulu on its path of ascension. We encountered Afxghelm two realms beyond the Sun. He was the last of his kind, ferocious-looking enough that all

---

48 The hologram of our previous location in the sky has been kept in place to avoid panic.

creatures avoided him. I was instructed to call sixty angels to sing him asleep as we moved through his realm.

Once we had moved through into the realms beyond, I was able to communicate with him. His first words to me were telepathically delivered, "Aren't you scared of me, too?" I told him I had heard that his species used to design plant forms and asked if we could be friends.

At first I got no reply. The masters instructed me to touch his tail, which was the customary way his species signaled their intent to initiate friendship. After doing so, I asked him to come to Earth and help design new plant forms to replace many that had been destroyed in the Amazon jungle. He seemed happy to not only have a friend, but to be useful again.

I contacted the nature god Pan and told him to warn the nature kingdoms not to be afraid of Afxghelm. I would tell the dragons. Pan offered to write a song about Afxghelm. Because he needed a cool, dark place to live, we decided he would live under the moist sand along the beach just west of my house.

Because of his proximity to the ocean, I contacted King Neptune and the queen of the water fairies, known only as Water Faye. King Neptune immediately asked if the first plants Afxghelm could design could be plants that absorb oil in the ocean.

Within three months this assignment was complete and the water fairies could implement it. This extraordinary, but true, tale of King Neptune had come full circle. The very 'monster' that had accidentally been the cause of his entrapment here was now collaborating with him to improve his kingdom.

Commentary on the Fifth Cycle

The reason the transition of many souls to the spirit world enhances the consciousness of those who are left behind, are as follows:

- How much consciousness we have depends on how much energy and other resources are at our disposal.
- Death empowers those in its presence, because the resources needed to sustain physical life is much more than that needed in the spirit world. The release of resources at the moment of death benefits those left behind.
- The two components of frequency are desire-based emotions (moving frequency), and little frequency bits as particles, creating patterns called states of being (static frequency). Memories determine the patterns. They are held in place by these patterns as well. It can be said that memories are the light component bonded to the frequency component (the little frequency particles).
- These memory patterns held in the states of being contaminate the pure expression of these states of being. They further tie up valuable resources in maintaining the memories. At death memories are released and resources become accessible to those left behind, raising their consciousness.

The Twelve Pure States of Being

Positive Aspect	Negative Aspect
Praise	Glory
Exploration	Harmony
Gratitude	Guidance
Discernment	Transparency
Understanding	Reflection
Embrace	Ecstasy
Manifestation	Inevitability
Oneness	Contentment
Integration	Evolution
Play	Flexibility
Perception	Power
Retention	Conductivity

The Twelve Pure Pairs of States of Being

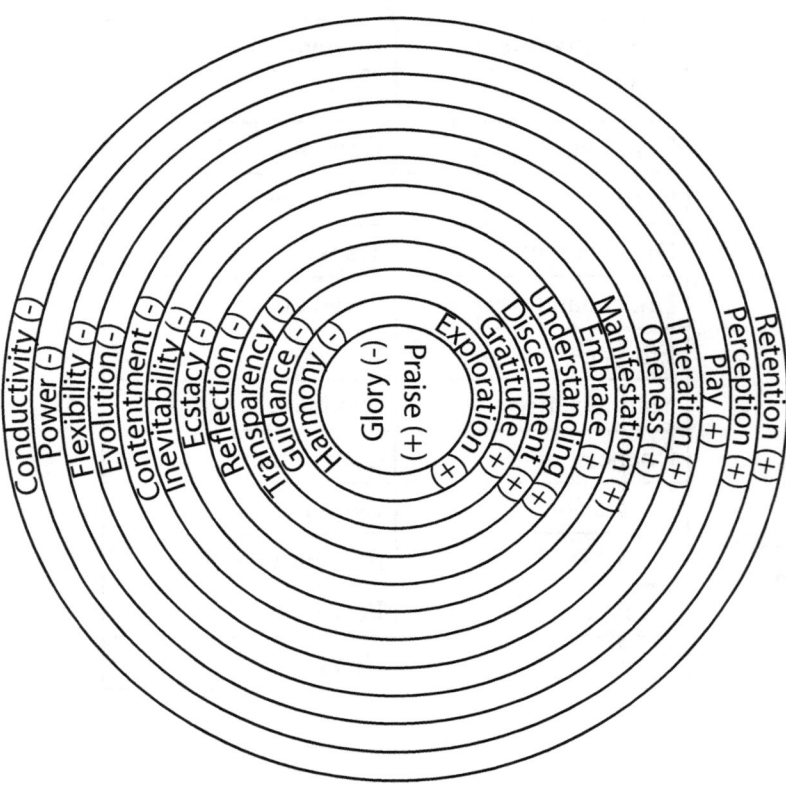

Each band represents a paired set of states of being.

Figure 21

The Twelve Pure Pairs of States of Being

1. **Praise** (+) As a state of being, Praise is slightly different than when it is an attitude. Attitudes have more perception. Praise is the surge of deep, exultant feeling that comes from seeing the highest aspect within something. It is the triumph of recognizing the perfection underlying appearances.

    Glory (-) Is the maintenance of the highest aspect of ourselves as a being as vast as the cosmos, and its expression in our lives. In other words, it's when we live life from our largest perspective.

2. **Exploration** (+) Is the pushing beyond previous boundaries of expression so that new creation and deeper expression can take place for the sake of growth.

    Harmony (-) Is the state of being resulting from being in step with the blueprint or will of the Infinite when smaller segments of Creation express synchronistically with the largest purpose of life.

3. **Gratitude** (+) This state of being results from encountering the true nature of the cosmos as one that supports all life; the recognition of the nurturing of the Divine in our lives.

    Guidance (-) Is the revelation of the most life-enhancing choices along our path and the uncovering of the blueprint of our existences.

    Note: Within the irrevocable overall purpose of our lives, there are now more choices and freedom of expression available than ever as we enter our spiritual maturity.

4. **Discernment** (+) Although all unknown portions of Mother's being have been solved during the cycles of the Fall, there is nevertheless always a mystery as to which expression of the

known portions of Her being would be most life-enhancing. The discernment comes when our hearts reveal this mystery.

Transparency (-) Is the revelation of a portion of existence that reflects the purity of absolute truth.

5. **Understanding** (+) When we regard our true identity as a being as vast as the cosmos, all is within our consciousness that is without our bodies. Understanding comes when the light-fibers within our bodies light up, or come on line, as a result of something outside our bodies revealing its information.

   Reflection (-) When something is encountered in life that evokes an emotional response, it is worthy of study and further scrutiny. It is an indicator of whether we have lived our highest truth. It may also be an indicator of a mystery waiting to reveal itself. Reflection will show whether what we understand is worthy of implementing and incorporating into our life.

6. **Embrace** (+) Is the reaching to incorporate more of the vastness of existence into our compassionate understanding and acceptance.

   Ecstasy (-) Results from the inclusiveness of our vision that sees each life as its own.

7. **Manifestation** (+) Fifty percent of life is ours to manifest and create at will; that part of life in which we can creatively contribute to the big picture. Manifestation occurs when awareness clusters itself into the circumstances of our lives, pulled forth by the emotions of our hearts, as well as our attitudes.

   Inevitability (-) Each of us plays a part in contributing to the growth and evolution of the large plan or pattern of life. This constitutes inevitability; the experiences we are required to live according to our mutual contract with the Infinite. Because growth comes through mutual support, the large plan also writes in some 'key moments'; variable moments of support in our own lives depending on which choices we make. This also is part of the set circumstances of our lives.

8. **Oneness** (+) Living the deep awareness that all beings are part of us makes us aware of the interconnectedness of life. We gain this understanding by opening ourselves to include all parts of existence.

   Contentment (-) This occurs when oneness occurs and life flows through us without obstruction. We feel that we have come home.

9. **Integration** (+) The praise-worthy parts of life beckon for us to make them our own - to integrate them as a part of us. That which we find unworthy of integrating, nevertheless has gifts in the form of insights that are worth making our own and should not be discarded.

   Evolution (-) As the caterpillar grows with each bite of the leaf it eats, so we grow in depth of wisdom and perception with each part of our experience we make our own and integrate. Change for the better is therefore the one constant in a life well lived.

10. **Play** (+) The spontaneous and lighthearted interaction with the unexpected creates a useful flexibility. It spontaneously and abundantly creates a grace and ease of interaction with life in the moment.

    Flexibility (-) The cumbersome weight of self-reflection, self-pity and self-importance weighs down the journey and keeps us locked into points of view. Any viewpoint must, in the next moment, be obsolete as life changes constantly, thought by thought.

11. **Perception** (+) Much abuse of power has occurred by reversing the polarity of power and perception. Power is the state of being

that results from perception, not the other way around. It is perception that must actively be sought in our world, not power.

Power (-) Power as a feminine pole is vastly more powerful than power that is masculine and separative. Power that is feminine and therefore inclusive in nature is the power that is aligned with all that is.

12. **Retention** (+) Whether to retain or allow something to flow through our lives requires our making a simple choice. The only real question in all existence is what is life-enhancing and what is not. That which is, we retain as our own.

    Conductivity (-) This state of being when fully lived, brings our lives into a state of grace. The alternative, resistance to that which we choose not to retain, leaks energy and lowers consciousness.

How the Emotions and States of Being Surround the Body

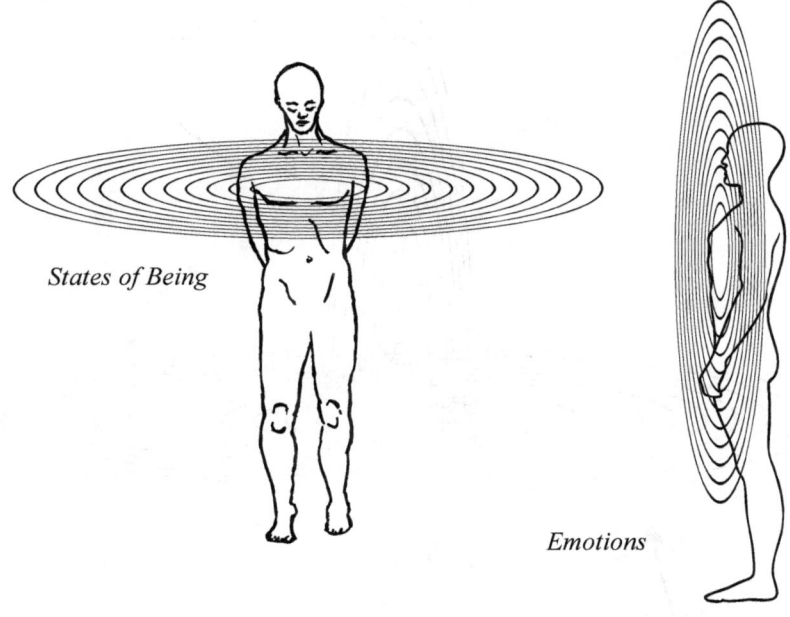

States of Being

Emotions

When both the Pure Emotions and the States of Being are fully pulsing and lived, the door in the heart opens and a feminine form of awareness is produced as we become co-creators. They dissect at their middle point through the heart.

Figure 22

How the Emotions and States of Being Intersect

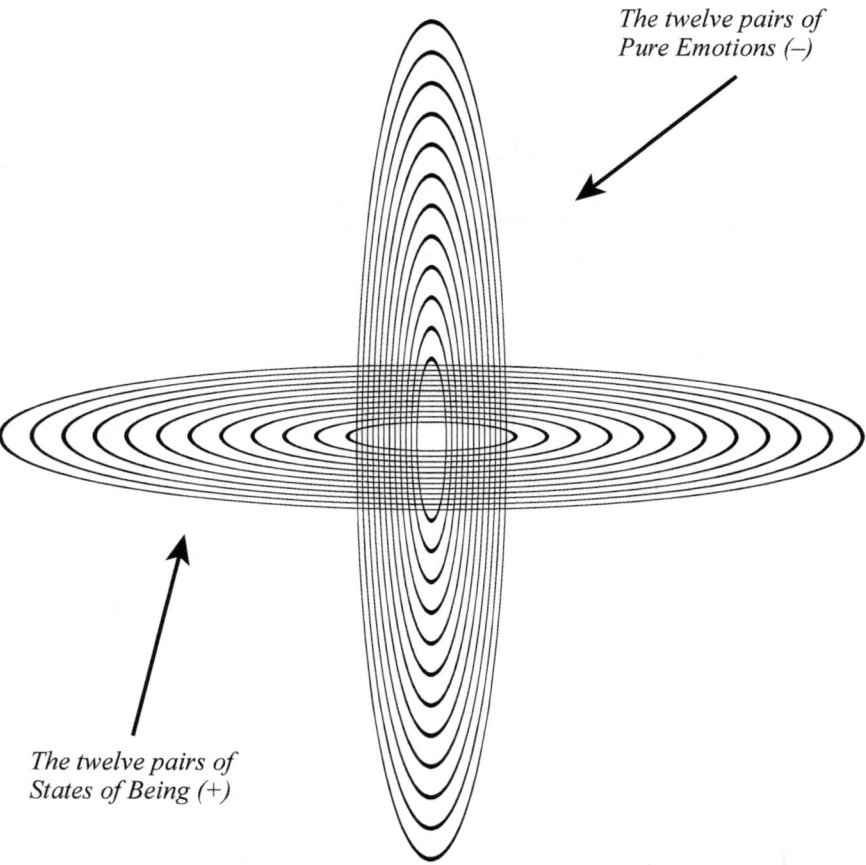

The rings each represent a pair that pulse between their positive and negative aspects. The wheels also pulse with each other. Although the emotions (frequency that moves) are feminine in relation to light, they are masculine in relation for the states of being that are more static.

Figure 23

Four Cycles Ago
Kluvarechshpi-urvavech

In the cycle before, and the one before
No longer the boy represented the Fall
The cycles were now embodied by a girl
Who dwelled within the inner Earth

Two cycles ago[49] she had been birthed
From Mother and a giant from the inner Earth
Egsplauvitpata her father had been
He guarded her well; immortal was she

The little girl was watching, waiting for change
Only then should she dwell upon the Earth's face
Kalima too, since the eighth cycle ago,
Mother had hidden in a pocket of space[50]

Now of the Annunaki we tell
Those who on the planet Nibiru dwell
At the end of the cycle known as eight
On Earth they had been miners, but leave did they

Those from Orion too here did mine
But they left the Earth at the end of cycle nine
The white powder they sought, they no longer could find
On Earth they leave the scars of their mines

The Annunaki did leave; their treaties dissolved
Because in the intrigue they didn't want to be involved

---

49 She had started representing the cycles during eight cycles ago. Six cycles ago she became their daughter.
50 She still hadn't shown herself in this cycle.

But during this cycle their atmosphere frayed[51]
They came here to mine and they came here to stay

The rise in frequency from five to four
Was much larger than the raises that happened before
Many cities and civilizations too
Completely disappeared, during the change, from view

The grip of the dark gods had lessened as well
So when the Annunaki on Earth came to dwell
They let them rule Egypt, India and Atlantis too
Eventually Africa, the Middle East and Europe too

Mother now ended Her stay far from Earth
Although She gave Herself memories from birth
She came into body as an adult
She had to change the whole family too as a result

A member of the ruling family She pretended to be
One of the Annunaki, it seemed, was She
The dark goddess followed, for it is clear
That wherever Mother went, she wanted to be near

Now a family member she pretended to be
Pretending to serve whenever Mother could see
Through slyness she undermined Mother's life
Unseen the dark god supported his wife

But Thoth too of that family pretended to be
He was not born and neither was she[52]
They pretended that brother and sister were they
Thoth had split himself, half unseen did stay

---

51 They needed to seal their atmosphere with Earth's gold.
52 The dark goddess of lies.

They each had a purpose; hers to deceive
Thoth from humanity more worship to receive
Mother intended the people to reach
She built many temples of the Goddess to teach

She had several palaces in which She could dwell
But she also traveled the people truths to tell
Enki, Thoth's 'father', a good man was he
But Thoth needed an ally and thus tampered with him

Mother's influence and Thoth's campaign
The dark gods noticed and intervened again
The energy from Mother's life force center drained
Was used by prophets who came forth that day

Tricks and miracles they did 'in the Father's name'
Teaching the people to the dark god to pray
From Nibiru a great avatar came
Mother loved him and wanted him as a mate

They had him killed, with the dark goddess's aid
They kept Her lonely and laughed at Her pain
Another who loved Mother Lemuria did rule
Sunat Kumara who established holy mystery schools

Her teachings and his, the people did raise
Their hearts to the Goddess did lift in praise
In the awake state, Mother didn't know who She was
She taught the divine feminine as it came through Her heart

No longer could the dark gods stand by
And see the light increase before their eyes
Numbers one, two and three together did stand
To implement a most diabolical plan

Tubes of gas under Lemuria lay
Which they did ignite; parts sank in a day
They hoped through the shock to cause a decline
Hoping that all into descension would slide

But though they killed the most conscious parts of man
It did not go exactly as planned
The more light someone holds, the more energy there is
As the light-filled die, the more energy released there is

Many the plans that had been made
The illuminated to kill, but the plans did now fade
The opposite resulted than what they sought
Bringing their destructive plans to naught

From martyrs' energy release to all
The cycle closed that was number four

Commentary on the Fourth Cycle

- It was during this cycle that the sub-personality of Wise Woman sank beneath the waves of conscious awareness. Represented by the sinking of Lemuria, the Earth lost its sub-personality too. The deserts grew, as much fertility was lost.
- Wise Woman represented the thirteen goddess archetypes. In their absence, the shallowness and lack of quality of life increased. The thirteen archetypes of the goddess create an alchemical equation that jointly form The Magical Existence of Divine Compassion.
- When parts of Existence are not fully expressing, artificial distortions take their place. In this way distortion grew among the goddesses.

The Thirteen Goddess Archetypes following the Suppression of Wise Woman

1. **PANA-TURA** Goddess of germination: the Mother. She is the essence of life-giving energy that births into form. She midwifes potentialities into materialization.

2. **AMA-TERRA-SU** Goddess of history. On earth she is the keeper of the history stored in the rocks, sand, and soil. She keeps the record of the loop of time, which is our biggest history.

3. **KA-LI-MA** Goddess of equity and destroyer of illusion. She brings balance by creating potentialities that can compensate for distortions that create karma.

4. **ORI-KA-LA** Goddess of prophecy with the farseeing eye. She is the oracle and holder of the key to changing the future.

5. AU-BA-RI Goddess of sound or frequency. She utilizes the rage of Lucifer to break up stagnant portions of Creation. She is the cosmic sound healer who works with the potential manifestation the spoken word creates.

6. HAY-HU-KA Goddess of reversal energy. She works with indwelling life's purpose to evolve awareness through manipulating the outer currents. She is the teacher who tricks others into learning.

7. ISHANA-MA Goddess of beauty, grace and elegance. She facilitates the peaceful interaction among her children for harmonious co-habitation. She is a mediator and promotes joyful cooperation. She is the goddess of self-love.

8. APARA-TURA Goddess of cycles. She is the operator who opens doors for cycles that are opening and closes doors for cycles that are closing. She celebrates the beginning and end of cycles.

9. HAY-LEEM-A Goddess of resources. She is the weigher of the consequences of today's actions on all life, including nature and future generations.

10. UR-U-AMA Goddess of creativity and inspiration. She knows true art inspires altered perception and that life should be lived creatively.

11. AMARAKU Goddess of new beginnings and forging new ways. When the old is gone, she invents a new approach. She is the innovator.

12. ALU-MI-NA Goddess who guards the unknowable. She guards the source of all spiritual knowledge from being accessed by those with impure motives. She is the gatekeeper who determines who may cross.

13. ARA-KA-NA Goddess of the power to transcend all boundaries. She is the guardian of the portal or passageway between Creator and Creation. She represents the gateway hidden within the core of human DNA that enables us to become the I AM that I AM.

The Thirteen Goddess Archetypes after the Restoration of Wise Woman

1. PANA-TURA – As the Embodiment of the Infinite births form through Divine Intent, this goddess midwives the tender, new beginnings of life. She is the one who nurtures with divine compassion the young of all species.

2. AMA-TERRA-SU – This goddess removes past memory patterns from awareness particles, and all other building blocks of life. She cleanses the pure states of being and all frequencies from the past's contaminations.

3. KA-LI-MA – She creates dynamic balance and flow, removing the blindness that causes value judgments. She removes perception blockages that create lack of reverence for all life, as well as that which obstructs seeing the perfection behind appearances.

4. ORI-KA-LA – She promotes living in the eternal fluid moment and dissolves ties of expectation that bind. She assists in self-empowered clarity and authentic living. She dissolves the illusion of the future.

5. AU-BA-RI – She helps to dissolve any illusions created by the spoken word. She dissolves programmed belief systems and clears the magnetic components of existence.

6. HAY-HU-KA – This goddess encourages humor and light-heartedness. She unfolds delightful synchronicities and joyously encourages optimism and a sense of adventure as we participate in life. She promotes unself-consciousness.

7. ISHANA-MA – Goddess of beauty, grace and elegance. She facilitates peaceful interaction and harmonious co-habitation. She is the goddess of enjoyment of existence.

8. APARA-TURA – She dissolves with grace, the illusions of space and linear becoming. She encourages joyful and trusting surrender to the Oneness of Life.

9. HAY-LEEM-A – She encourages a life of no opposites, so that we may overcome the limited resources available within polarity by becoming one with Source.

10. UR-U-AMA – Goddess of creativity and inspiration. She knows life can be a living work of art and creativity, to enhance the quality of the journey.

Book II – Freedom from the Treadmill

11. AMARAKU – She is the goddess of spontaneous and authentic expression. She encourages the surrendered trust that allows Infinite existence to unfold through us with ease and grace.

12. ALU-MI-NA – The revealer of the ever-receding horizon of self-perception, she encourages humility and child-like wonderment at the exquisite perfection that is ever new.

The Lemurian Science of Peace

13. ARA-KA-NA – The goddess of the open heart of divine, all-encompassing compassion. She encourages boundless inclusiveness and deep, abiding peace.

The Third Cycle Ago
Mirvanadochstra-uvabach

When the fourth cycle ended
The dark god took credit
"Believe in me and I will save you
From the awful things that can befall you"

As the cycles rose to number three
Few Annunaki remained to be seen
Some ascended through the sun
From the changes the lower ones were gone

Isis, immortal, remained behind
Except Enki and Thoth she was the last of her kind
Why then had Enki and Thoth not died?
And the dark goddess too remained behind?

Number One dark god and also Thoth
Energy sources hid for him and the dark goddess both
To awaken the pattern and restore their life
Thoth helped Enki, the dark god, his wife

Thoth tapped into the Earth's life force
Enki too did use this source
Osiris too wanted to incarnate
But they prevented him, his light was too great

Thoth impressed the people with his immortality
Humans too tried to simulate the Annunaki
With the overlords gone, arrogant kings arose
But some were good who sat upon thrones

Throughout this cycle Thoth's arrogance grew
To win support he traveled the cosmos through
He no longer felt threatened by the rising light
He thought if he wanted he could suppress it with might

The dark gods had started to damage each other
Just like they had done before to the Mother
But Thoth ignored them—what did he care?
They couldn't harm him. They wouldn't dare!

But strike they did, in fact times three
Atlantis destroyed and sunk into the sea

First of Atlantis, but islands remained
The second time two islands, Ruta and Itaya were named
The third time a landmass Poseidonis called
But it too before their anger did Fall

Thoth had gathered star technology
But it did not prevent these catastrophes
From these disasters energy released
Raising the consciousness, the dark gods were displeased

They should have learnt from cycles before
That with more light, more energy is stored
But their judgement could not their anger stay
Thus very foolishly acted did they

Thoth knew who Mother was during this time
But She still did not know that She was divine
Her damage in the ninth cycle sustained
Still in this cycle with Her remained

The dragons were angry that what had been said
In the form of promises had not been kept
Mother found more happiness and peace in these days
And so to another cycle the cosmos did raise.

Commentary on the Third Cycle

- The sinking of Atlantis, created the suppression of the Inner Sage and the god-facets that he represents. Because he was not being expressed, yet again artificial distortions filled the abandoned areas: He became a power seeker instead of a perception seeker.[53]

---

53 See *A Life of Miracles*.

The Twelve God Orders following the Inner Sage's Suppression

1. **LA-U-MI-EL** Lord of all consciousness. The symbol is the hieroglyph for reciprocity, also used to indicate wisdom in harvesting. This lord works with the law of compensation in nature to bring about the balanced evolution of species.

2. **AKASHA-EL** Lord of the Akashic records and keeper of history. He is also the keeper of the spoken word and language. He determines the insights of history by being the holder of the big picture. The symbol means permanent record.

3. **KARAMA** Lord of karma. He determines where karma can best be learned and experienced. The symbol stands for the opening of all 12 chakras, which only occurs when a being has removed the seals of unresolved karma by learning the lessons past experience teaches.

4. **URI-EL** Lord of intelligence. He is the interpreter of insights gained and redesigns the evolution of awareness accordingly. He turns information through intelligence into the known.

5. **KI-AS-MUS** Lord of time and space. He works within the allotted amount of time to evolve awareness within a certain space (in Creation, time and space have established limits).

6. **MI-RA-EL** Lord of symbols of hidden knowledge (includes DNA coding). He determines what must be hidden and what must be revealed within DNA coding or through symbols. He also works with pivotal energy.

7. **OM-KA-EL** Lord who holds the vision. He creates the template that fulfills the purpose of a certain part of creation. The symbol stands for focus and will, or focused intent.

8. **KA-PA-EL** Lord of the cycles. He works with the cycles of change all life goes through: transformation, transmutation, and transfiguration. The spiral is either positive, resulting in a higher form of the life form, or negative, resulting in death.

9. **LEEM-U-EL** Lord of the flow of awareness. He oversees the interaction of the different forms of awareness during the in- breath and out-breath of God—the large creational cycles.

10. ILLUMINATI Lord of illumination. He creates the grid lines along which creation will be formed. He is the architect and engineer for wielding sacred geometry.

11. KU-MA-RA Lord of hierarchy and government. He brings stability through structure to growth. He represents the perfect balance between the neutral, feminine and masculine elements.

12. KA-LI-SA Lord of energy distribution. He determines the amount of energy a life form can hold.

The Twelve God Orders after the Inner Sage's Restoration

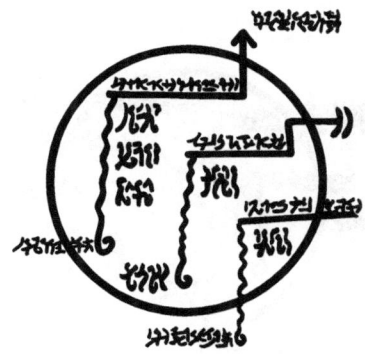

1. **LA-U-MI-EL** – The god of the eternal perspective. He promotes living from timelessness and the knowingness of ourselves as infinite beings.

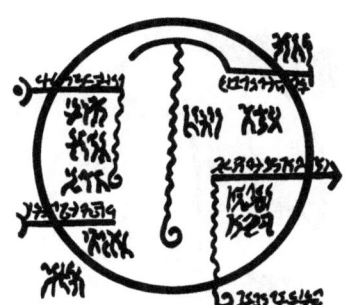

2. **AKASHA-EL** – God of exponential expression. He eliminates the illusions of cause and effect and closes down space created by linear change. He helps us hear the answer within the question.

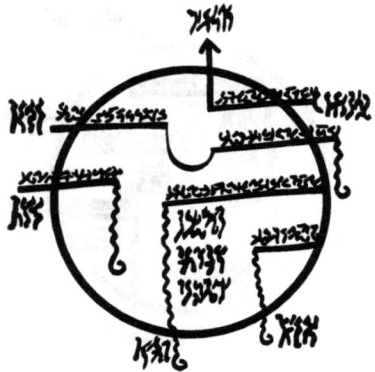

3. KARAMA – The god who sees the purity of experience. All that exists serves a purpose or it would not exist at all. In acknowledging the value of all things, life becomes supportive rather than adversarial.

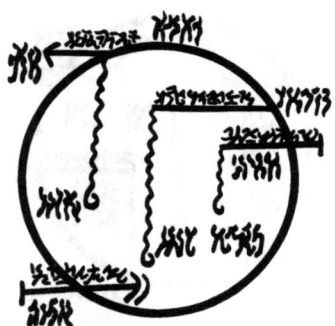

4. URI-EL – The god of effortless knowing and the dissolving of the tools of mind. He reminds us of the ability to achieve genius by living in mindlessness. He sees no guilt, because there are no choices other than how we respond to life.

Book II – Freedom from the Treadmill

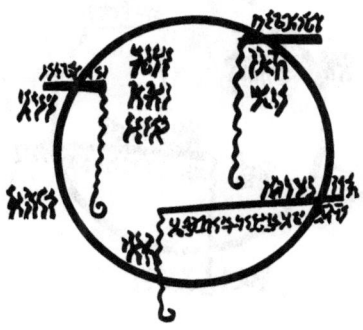

5. KI-AS-MUS – The god of dancing with the contradiction. This god eliminates the addiction of knowing, of having to label our environment. He knows all life is unknowable and that all renews itself every moment.

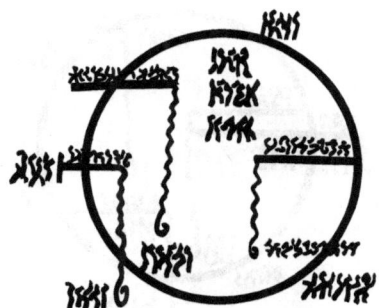

6. MI-RA-EL – The god of cancelling all contracts and agreements. The only course of action is to live from the authentic expression of the fullness of our being, free from the expectations of others.

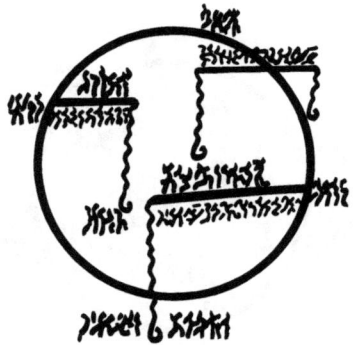

7. OM-KA-EL – The god that dissolves all tyrannies through understanding. This god promotes self-empowerment by knowing ourselves to be portals of expression for the One Life.

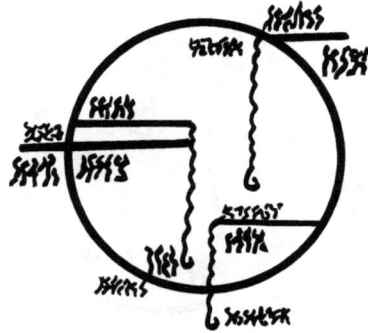

8. KA-PA-EL – The god of eternal transcendence. He dissolves any weight of self-reflection, or entanglements of duality. He promotes fluidly changing omni-perspective.

Book II – Freedom from the Treadmill

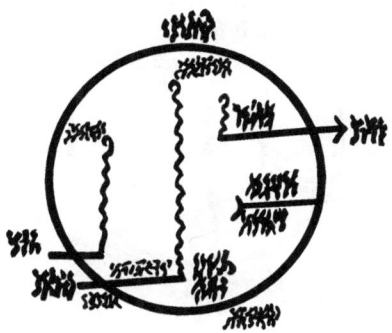

9. LEEM-U-EL – The god of peaceful transitions through fluid surrender. He embraces changeless change and fluid cooperation with the newness of unfolding life.

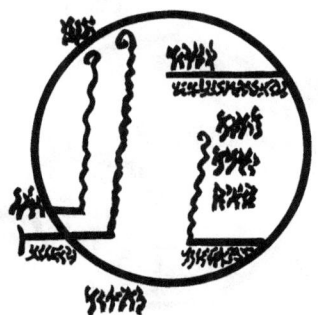

10. ILLUMINATI – The god of no relationships. He advocates the deep knowing that life is indivisible, and the recognition that another is but ourself hiding from ourselves.

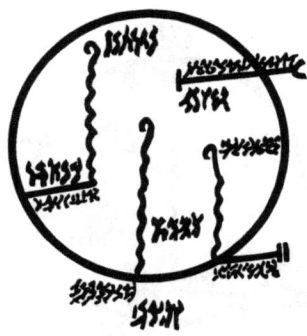

11. KU-MA-RA – The god of genderless existence. When all tension that is the result of gender interaction is removed, we enter motionless motion, the contradiction where everything is eternal yet expresses anew every moment.

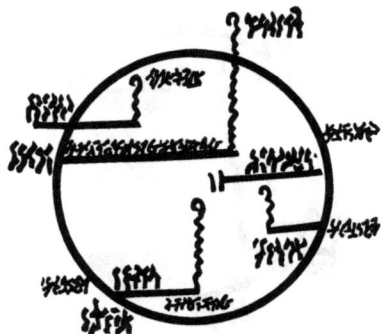

12. KA-LI-SA – The god of miracles of the unified field. This is the dissolving of the illusions that have contributed to linear change: body, soul and formless spirit. Knowing ourselves to be an ever-unfolding emphasis within the field of life is the beginning of miracles.

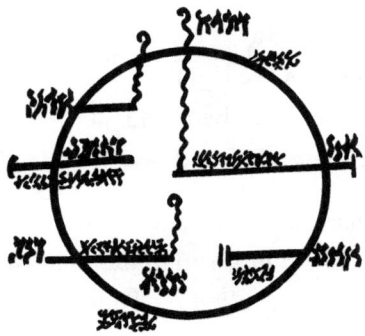

13. NA-KA-AL – The impeccable seer and spiritual warrior. The one who lives from an open heart and highest vision, living from humble surrender. Together the 13 gods form the alchemical equation of: A life of no opposites through humble surrender.

Two Cycles Ago
Kluavivachvrasteruvit

Mother felt the time was right
In the lower levels to boost the light
A drastic choice would have to be made
She Herself would come to their aid

Since light had increased and awareness arose
A great ascension could occur through the plan She chose
For support for this plan she relied on Thoth
In fact, upon him and the dark goddess both

She still did not know that they were dark
She still for them had love in Her heart
She still did not know who She or they were
Only that the people's well-being depended upon Her

She decided from the palace one level above
To enter the physical world of the people She loved
This would mean forgetfulness and suffering to bear
But Thoth assured Her that with aid he would be there

Illusion weighted the cosmos down
It still persisted no matter how many seeds of light She'd sown
If She entered physicality and ceased to forget
Illusion would be broken, ascension to abet

The dark goddess insisted that devoted was she
That she never Mother's side would leave
Mother wanted to spare her the pain that would be there
She insisted that no sacrifice was too big to bear

She wanted as Mother's daughter to come in
But Mother's womb could not hold so dark an energy
As Mother walked in to an adult body, so did she
By changing families' memories

There was supposed to be a memory of childhood
Mother would have, but that she would later remember the truth
Thus She came in, as an adult to live
Through Her overcomings, ascension to give

Thoth helped Her leave but then moved in
He lived in Her palace with his harem
He barred Her dreambody from returning home
No further aid given, She was truly alone

Nightmares plagued Her of a home She'd lost
She wanted to return even at a high cost
She finally realized Her home is within
And that's when ascension did rapidly begin

When She entered among humankind
Two lives She lived to effectively use time
She entered one life forward to live
The other went back in time neither there was She birthed

The life back in time in England transpired
A death was staged; in a plane crash She pretended to expire
The dark goddess also part of a family pretended to be
By the other dark goddess assisted was she

Finally Mother remembered Her task
Preparations for ascension She made at last
The dark ones all entered her life to be
Advisors who professed to help Her see

The Number One dark god to Lucifer did sell
The elves, and half the fairies, if he helped him as well
The re-location of these kingdoms to where they belong
Was done by Mother to right this wrong

Through the Fall's many cycles frustration grew[54]
Deep within Mother for She never knew
Why Her feminine aspects didn't help Her more
She didn't remember the three She had hidden before

She didn't know how diluted they were
She thought they were equal matches to Her
Out of frustration a decision was honed
Henceforth She would carry the cosmos alone

She started now preparations to make
To raise the cosmos, to open the gates
In the beginning Her life was plagued
Hostile aliens did Her life invade

For through Earth's ascension they could plainly see
That their repressive races would soon cease to be
Thoth had shown them where the special one
The girl child lived, for on the surface she'd come

But throughout this cycle, page by page
For within each cycle, pages divide the age
The hostile races abducting human beings
Through frequency raises ceased to be

---

54 During the cycles when She still knew who She was.

The Lords of Amenti, now there were nine
Were wanting more power, abiding their time
They were alarmed at Mother's success
They wanted to control Her, just like the rest

When Mother called a million souls home
Who'd been abducted, taken to alien homes
Their joy was great to Earth to return
The frequency rose as they entered the spirit world

The spirit worlds, where the departed dwell
Were united, the ascended masters' realms to
    spirits opened as well
Mother gave to all beings a feeling body to use
"Use it or through ascension your life you'll lose"

But the dragons still fumed in their hidden world
For once more a dragon named Hy a wall did build[55]
Thoth made sure that Mother as an enemy was seen
Does she not threaten the dragon's repressive regime?

Thus a rebellion by them was staged
A cosmic war they planned to wage
They intimidated many with their rage
To depose the leader, the nine lords thought safe

A two-year-old dragon was called to the post
But the deposed leader continued threatening most
With but hours to spare before the war
The Earth rose higher than it was before

---

55 See *Secrets of the Hidden Realms* for a full account of the dragon's rebellion.

This rise in consciousness was high indeed
It killed one-tenth of those who would not heed
Mother remembered at last who She was
And because of that raised the whole cosmos

The Lords Called to Represent the Coming Together of the Spirit Realms

The Five Lords of Duat *(previously the lower spirit worlds)*

1. ***Set-hampotep***
   He represents: Positive pole – Discipline
   Negative pole – Warmth
   He overcomes the illusion of Emptiness.

2. ***Lumurian Hokepah***
   He represents: Positive pole – Vision
   Negative pole – Determination
   He overcomes the illusion of Inertia.

3. ***Humka***
   He represents: Positive pole – Impeccability
   Negative pole – Integrity
   He overcomes the illusion of Egotism.

4. ***Sumara-el***
   He represents: Positive pole – Sobriety
   Negative pole – Clarity
   He overcomes the illusion of Judgement.

5. ***Zoraed***
   He represents: Positive pole – Objectivity
   Negative pole – Discretion
   He overcomes the illusion of Dishonesty.

The Five Lords of Sekhet-Hepspet *(the higher spirit world)*

1. *Merchanda*
   He represents: Positive pole – Discipline
   Negative pole – Strength
   (There was less illusion in *Sekhet-Hepspet*)

2. *Umvatba Ulara*
   He represents: Positive pole – Vision
   Negative pole – Focus

3. *Tasalmonis*
   He represents: Positive pole – Impeccability
   Negative pole – Harmlessness

4. *Aranandame*
   He represents: Positive pole – Sobriety
   Negative pole – Interpretation

5. *Ptalomatis*
   He represents: Positive pole – Objectivity
   Negative pole – Discernment

When these lords combined their energies, they represented the principle of Divine Compassion.

The new angel Mother called to represent the Earth's spirit world was *Alamundara*.

The One Lord Who Guarded the Portal to the Ascended Master's Realms was *Ratmatorama-atmaset*.

The Lemurian Sigil of the Combined Spirit Worlds

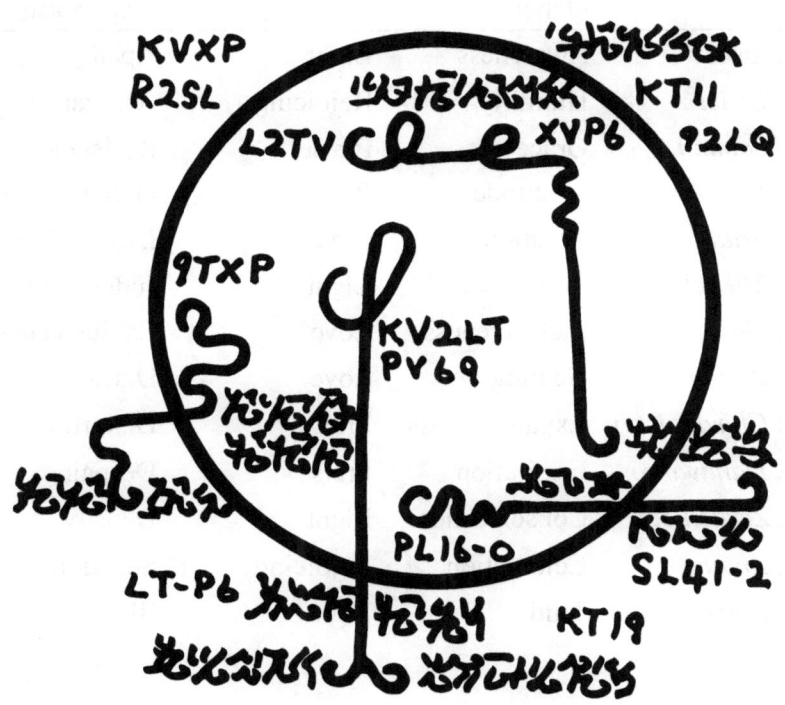

Figure 24

The Thirteen High Angels Who Guarded the Veil to the Ascended Master's Level

Name	Meaning of their work	Attribute embodied	The illusion they banish
1. *Aviel*	Awareness	Light	Apathy
2. *Urfiel*	Humility	Rejoicing	Arrogance
3. *Salmon*	Grace	Praise	Resistance
4. *Bath Qol*	Gratitude	Rejoicing	Greed
5. *Elian*	Creation	Love	Destruction
6. *Mikael*	Intelligence	Light	Judgement
7. *Gabriel*	Inclusiveness	Love	Exclusiveness
8. *Raphael*	Healing	Love	Disease
9. *Chirangiyah*	Expansiveness	Praise	Distortion
10. *Dahavauron*	Inspiration	Praise	Despair
11. *Zerachiel*	Consciousness	Light	Density
12. *Abauw*	Celebration	Rejoicing	Self-doubt
13. *Eblis*	Truth	Light	Illusion

The Merkaba-Fields of Existence

Around the bodies of beings and the cosmos, there have been the following fields, the different geometric shapes of which get progressively larger:

A. **Three star-tetrahedrons** (three-dimensional Stars of David). One is stationary, one spins clockwise and one counterclockwise at the ratio of 34 times for every 21 times the clockwise one spins. They all occupy the same space.

B. **Three octahedrons** (two four-sided pyramids base-to-base). Just like before, these three occupy the same space with one stationary and two spinning in opposite directions at a specific ratio (the ratios follow the Fibonacci sequence).

C. **Three dodecahedrons** (twelve pentagons in the shape of a soccer ball). Just like before, they occupy the same space, one stationary, one spinning left and one spinning right.

D. **Three Flower of Life spheres.** Each of the shapes previously mentioned occupy larger and larger areas around the body. Those beings that chose not to feel have two stationary fields and one counterclockwise spinning field. Their fields that should spin clockwise are stationary. These did not survive the ascension. In the case of beings that cannot feel, the Flower of Life spheres have a deformity in the spheres themselves in that, as seen from the front, the right-hand portion of the spheres are incomplete in each of the three fields. During the ascension this was corrected for all beings.

Some time during the 18th cycle ago, the Merkabic fields were tampered with to produce left-brain dominance in all life. This produced separation consciousness. The electric (counter-clockwise spinning) mental fields were made to spin faster, whether around a planet, a cosmos or a human body. This created mental dominance over the emotional ability to access subtle information.

Those who live from the star-tetrahedrons are in identity-consciousness. Those who live from the octahedral fields are in god-consciousness (expanded awareness). Those who live from the dodecahedral fields are in immortal mastery.

The Fields of Godhood

Beings, the cosmos and planets have three perfect Flower of Life spheres around their bodies.

1. There needs to be 19 perfectly interwoven circles in each Flower of Life sphere.
2. All fields associated with the emotional and mental bodies should be spinning in the right direction and in the appropriate ratio and speeds.
3. When a being goes beyond immortality into godhood, he or she lives from the Flower of Life spheres.

Perfect Flower of Life Sphere

Figure 25

Commentary on the Second Cycle

- During the second cycle, the presence of the Embodiment among men was instrumental in allowing those of higher consciousness to live from a different level of reality; the octahedral fields. It is for this reason that She embodied as two; one living from the star-tetrahedrons, the other from the octahedrons.
- The tube torus of existence became larger (the octahedrons occupy a larger space) and many new realms were incorporated into the cosmos.

New Species Incorporated into the Cosmos

Little known kingdoms with huge magical abilities were hidden by Mother in pockets of space outside the cosmic boundaries during the fourteenth cycle ago. Each kept specific frequencies of the cosmos. She did not want the kings and dark ones to appropriate these for themselves. These kingdoms incorporated when we expanded as a cosmos and joined us during the third week of April 2007.

The Ellamakusanek

April 17, 2007

Like the Darklings, the Ellamakusanek are very diminutive and live in large numbers in the bottom of the ocean. Left in the void in what appeared to be a very dark indigo rectangular-shaped space, they slept in a type of stasis in order to conserve whatever energy they had until Mother remembered about them and it was safe for them to come out.

Those who lost hope died, but 20% of them also rebelled not believing that Mother would come for them. Sadly, those who had turned against Mother were not permitted into the cosmos.

The Ellamakusanek are like little spheres of light with a tiny form inside – a little like very diminutive fairies. They are more ethereal than the Darklings. Apparently they emit light that grows brighter when they are happy. They live in large family groups and love to be gathered together.

The Ellamakusanek speak in sounds resembling the squeaks of mice to our ears. They are called the bringers of hope. That with which Mother entrusted them is the ability to repair and re-program DNA, as well as increase chromosomes and put new information for a huge evolutionary leap into the life force center.

In the case of all three of these kingdoms, their contributions of frequency are part of producing a 'super-charged' human of higher consciousness.

The Bekbavarabishpi

April 18, 2007

I saw the Bekbavarabishpi clearly and recognized them at once from their artwork that had been part of the intricate and sometimes large wheels[56]. I was told by Mother to construct as tools to open the membranes between the realms as the Earth started to ascend in February 2005. As we have seen, during some of the cycles within the Fall, the Earth either tore or bounced off a membrane when a gateway hadn't been created for her passage.

The Bekbavarabishpi originated in ancient Lemuria (called Shalmali at the time). Sometime before they were hidden by Mother fourteen cycles ago, they forsook living among the rest of the population in favor of living among the trees in heavily forested areas. They became known as the Tree People.

They had, and still have, the ability to materialize and de-materialize at will, sometimes entering into trees to hide. I asked why they had withdrawn from society; the answer was, "The trees are kinder."

There are 986 of them that returned to Earth on the date given above. I asked if, like the Ellamakusanek, any portion of them had lost faith and been unable to return into the cosmos. The answer came very quickly; "All love Mother. All here."

They live in caves or stone houses. I asked whether their stone houses were round or square like ours; "Round only when a cave." They are vegetarians. Their clothes are made from tree bark, but look more pliable and thinner than the bark 'cloth' called tapa, made by South Sea Islanders.

Physically their appearance is the epitome of refinement. Their build and features are delicate and well formed. They have very light blond hair, almost white in fact, and gentle, pale blue eyes. The adults stand

---

56 See Part I, *Secrets of the Hidden Realms*.

between 20-22 feet tall. The initial contact with them was with a family of four: parents, an older daughter and younger son.

I was told they were very much hunted after Mother hid them because of the gifts they carried that pertain to sight. "You mean the ability to see realms above the one we're in?" I asked. "There are more ways to 'see' than that!" I asked for an example. "To see underneath what is happening." I asked whether they meant to see behind the appearances. "No, what's going on underneath." I didn't quite understand but didn't press them further.

Their gifts are given by activating certain parts of the brain, as I later found out after a rather acute, raving headache. But I got the impression something was also done to the etheric lenses in the front and behind the eyes. My eyes were swollen and bloodshot after their work on me, which took place two nights later. Like the other kingdoms, they were preparing us for higher consciousness and their gifts were for everyone.

The rectangular pocket of space the Ellamakusanek were in was such a dark indigo as to appear almost navy blue. The Bekbavarabishpi's pocket of space was, on the other hand, kite-shaped and the color of the throat chakra. The darker sky blue became lighter as they came closer to the cosmos. At all times during our interactions with them, they emanated a deep and gentle love.

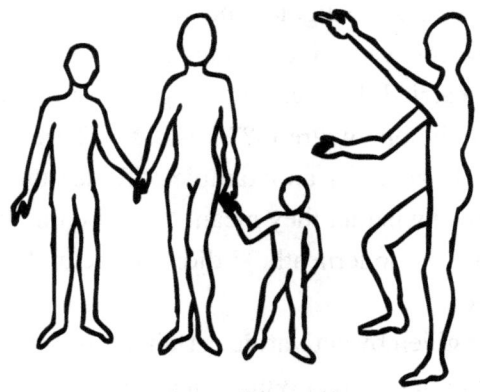

The Bekbavarabishpi

The father is explaining to his family that during the steps up of the cosmic ascension, when the earth has moved from here to there, the Bekbavarabishpi shall emerge.

Figure 26

The Nitzkabelavek

April 19, 2007

Before the Nitzkabelavek actually arrived, they had appeared telepathically on Earth. During the construction of the wheels in 2005, they had appeared to me in a dream to give me their symbols that had to be only a specific wheel, or cosmic gate.

The Nitzkabelavek are between two and two-and-a-half feet in height and either go naked or wear very few clothes. The leader wore a turban-like headpiece to indicate his status.

When the Nitzkabelavek do wear clothes, they mostly consist of just one piece; a pair of pants, for example. The only clothes I saw were made of feathers. They live in hollowed-out areas under trees. During the week, the fairies permitted me into their world for the writing of

Arubafirina—The Book of Fairy Magic. I had seen the inside of many of their homes. They had primitive but detailed furniture with many useful household items not dissimilar to some of ours.

The Nitzkabelavek's homes have the barest minimum. Their 'bed' may be a piece of hollow bark covered with moss and feathers. Not much trouble is taken to produce their furniture.

Their little bodies are rounded like those of toddlers and the impression of their being 'childlike' is enhanced by their small, round, hairless heads. Their faces have an owlish appearance because of the large eyes and pronounced brow ridges that become long, narrow, beak-like noses. Their mouths are very small.

These little beings brought the gift of specific frequencies as well. All of the Nitzkabelavek who were hidden have returned, and there are between 1,500-2,000 of them. They are able to teleport themselves wherever they wish to go within moments—a special gift of this kingdom.

The Nitzkabelavek
Their pronounced brow ridges that form into a long beak-like, skinny nose, as well as their large eyes, give them an owlish appearance. They are 2 to 2½ feet tall.

Figure 27

Other Major Events Coinciding with the Return of the Lost Kingdoms

It was as though the contributions of the Lost Kingdoms put part of a puzzle together and Mother did the rest. The picture of the puzzle was one of an end to ages of darkness and suppression and of a new dawning of light for all life.

As the Lost Kingdoms did their part, Mother and other gods and goddesses did the rest:
- The restoration of the true colors of the twelve DNA strands (they consist of sub-atomic particles) activated a specific cell in the pineal gland. Discovered by scientists in those known as 'avatars', or those having marked extra-sensory gifts, it has been called the god-cell.
- The core of the Earth had been very slowly spinning clockwise. It was made to spin counterclockwise at the optimum speed. This raised planetary consciousness and transfigured old memories kept there.
- The brainstem in humans had a clockwise spin in the fields around the cells. This was reversed, raising consciousness and releasing old memories.

One Cycle Ago
Elvishvraklarespi

Mother with earnest, as in the cycle before
To Her etheric palace tried to open the door
Many the false deadlines and promises too
Were given to Her by advice untrue

Many times prematurely did the kingdoms rejoice
Too often for naught in praise did they raise their voice
"The dark ones are gone, deceit is no more!
There is no need to suffer as we did before"

The dark ones encouraged expectations like these
Another disappointment would only bring Mother grief
Why did they pretend to help with the palace at all?
To create disappointment and to falsely declare an end to the Fall

By saying the Fall is over when really it was not
Could make Mother with Her improvements of the cosmos stop
By letting Her think She did succeed
They could bring disappointment by undoing Her deeds

If they wore Her down with the tasks assigned
Surely eventually She'd give up in time
Taking directions at the imposter's behests
Mother at the instructions grew more perplexed

But then the three feminine aspects She'd left behind
The ones who were in hiding since the beginning of time
Contacted Her as to the top[57] we had come
In joyous reunion with Her they became one

She removed the imposter from what was Her place
The one who had, to look like Her, assumed Her face
The imposters to the Grand Realms blocked the way
But neither at the top of the cycles could the cosmos stay[58]

Many the gods who in these days
Forsook the Mother and a higher way
Behind the illusion of Earth's night sky[59]
Twelve planetary systems around the Earth did lie

The Pleiades, Lyra, Antares too
Arcturus, to name but a few
All twelve gods darkness chose
Their planets to Earth could no longer be close

As they the Earth long ago expelled
Now it was their turn to be repelled
The holiest place the Earth had become
On the Earth dwelled the Holy One

Now Mother created twelve planets anew
To study the wisdom Earth has accrued
To teach the wisdom to other stars
The Earth's glory would be known near and far

---

57 The top of the cycles of the Fall.
58 This would have caused stagnation.
59 The sky has changed but to prevent fear, an illusion is kept in place.

> *The star systems are given in the order Mother created them are, in the star languages:*
>
> | | |
> |---|---|
> | Sfadurchptapr | Gir |
> | Hmtoupeex | Topf |
> | Fngtfs | Mcbstfre |
> | Labiyz | Dopsisssssv |
> | Tttv | Aiiqxqwqiii |
> | Aeyaioauiauieuai | Home (pronounced H<u>o</u>-me') |
>
> *The first six systems study the wisdom of the Earth. The next six systems teach it to other star systems.*

But secretly Her dreambody a parallel cosmos prepared
The cosmos could go sideways if it couldn't go ahead
A portal prepared, around it physical gods stood
The cosmos pulled through a shield, permitting only good

Not the first time it was Mother used this ploy
To bypass a trap, their dark plans to foil
At the end of the third cycle with opposition ahead
She took this planet over the edge of space instead

As the Earth then ascended, pulling all behind
Thus again Mother made a plan of the same kind
All should've succeeded, how could it not be?
Then why were the dark ones once again seen?

By traveling through tunnels in between realms
Mother could visit higher Mothers there
Far did she travel to levels far beyond
To seek out how answers could be found

Forty and four levels up was the last feminine aspect of Her
Beyond that consciousness lay, in all directions, forever
To this high goddess Mother wisdom did impart
"Search for treachery in the God of Truth's heart"

Great was the grief the Mother then knew
The heart of Her love held only untruth
They traveled back[60] to before his creation
With the forty-fourth goddess they shared this realization:

We come from your future, do not do this deed
Earnestly consider and to our words give heed
Let him ever uncreated be
No offspring shall he sire, filled with lies and greed

Though hearts did bleed from all the feminine aspects below
Uncreated the perpetrators were and so
Finally the cycles of the Fall did end
This time for real; no more pretence

Everyone's lives now must change
For the blueprint of life itself has changed[61]
Do not hold on to old patterns of fear
Lift up your eyes. The reign of the Mother is here.

Commentary on the First Cycle

- The dance of illusion is still prevalent when life is lived from either the star-tetrahedron or the octahedron, in that life is based on relationships. The Embodiment of the Infinite still sees Her

---

60 The sixth feminine aspect above us traveled with her.
61 Deeper insights into the cycles of the Fall can be found in *Opening the Doors of Heaven*.

feminine aspects as parts of Her She had externalized. In fact they were mirror images reflected in the mirrored confinements (geometry) of embodiment – the boundaries that define an individuation.
- This can be said two ways: Firstly, mirror images are the backwards images of an individual that move when he or she moves. Secondly, there are no real mirrors, because existence is indivisible – they are just the result of a pretended self-relationship through self-reflection.
- In the same way, the dodecahedral fields mirror the illusion of seeing archetypal aspects without: the god and goddess archetypes.
- These three sets of fields represent the shell of the incubation egg of the cosmos and its contents. The natural state of life is godhood – the Flower of Life sphere (19 spheres within the 20th). The stages of identity consciousness, god-consciousness or expanded awareness, or immortal mastery, are but the accentuating of certain of the spheres of the Flower of Life (godhood's facets).
- In identity-consciousness, 7 of the inner spheres are 'on line', and the 13 goddess archetypes join as one with the 13 god archetypes, forming the rest of the Flower of Life sphere ($7 + 13 = 20$).
- In the life of one in a higher consciousness, 8 of the spheres within the Flower of Life sphere are 'on line' and expressing, but now there are only 12 god and goddess archetypes that are joined and expressing. The 13th god/goddess expression is removed, ($12 + 8 = 20$).
- The reason for this is that for one in identity consciousness or ego-identity, the gateway to Source through the Embodiment of the Infinite is blocked, because they behave egocentrically in a way that benefits only the small self. The 13th god and goddess block the way by providing limited guidance and resources.

- Egocentricity sees life as being 'without'. The higher consciousness sees life as 'within'. The attempts to control life to benefit the smaller self is in a broad sense black magic. Black magicians have limited power. The viewpoint of seeing life as 'within', creates white magic; changing life as we change ourselves. It has the power of all creations (being seen as the self) to draw from.

Creating an Alternate Route of Ascension

The Sea of Consciousness

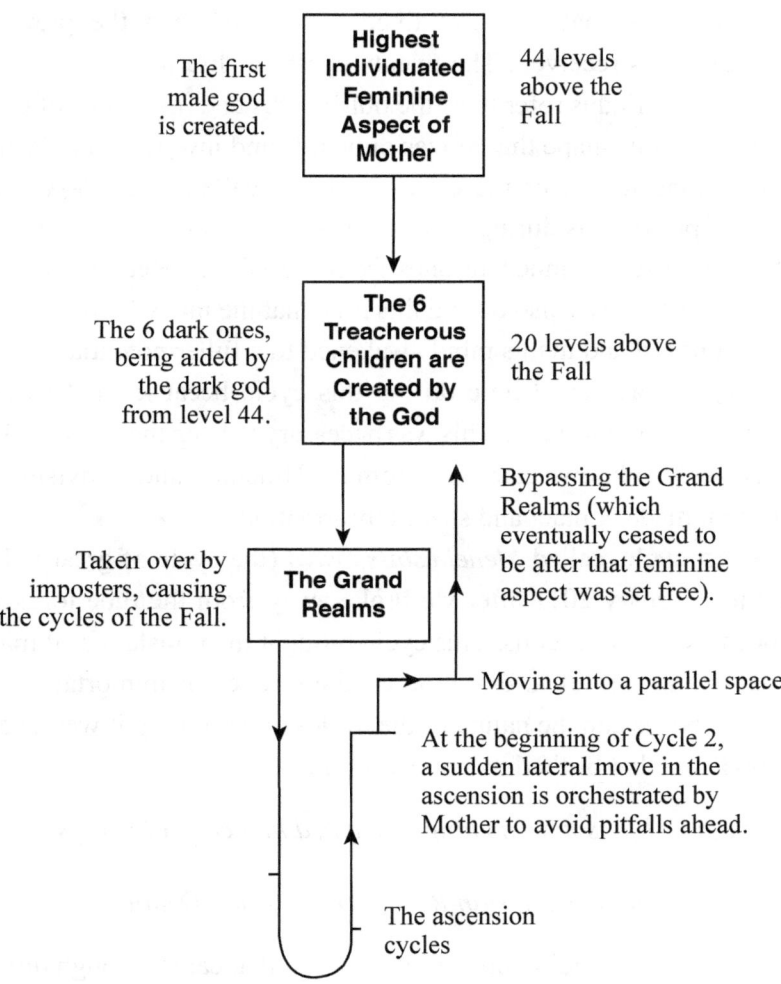

Twenty levels above the Fall, the six distorted gods and goddesses were created solely by the god.

Figure 28

Closing on the History of the Cycles

There have been an additional two cycles that were part of a twenty-cycle 'treadmill' that we have lived – beyond when the previous information was received. The twenty cycles of life formed the giant tube torus the Hindus refer to as the out-breaths and in-breaths of God: A huge doughnut shape that moves outwards and inwards upon itself.

The second to last of these two cycles is called *Menech-pahuva*, the age of purity. It is during this time that the Earth saw the return of the Kachina tribes – innocent ones from the Hidden Realms that had been in hiding. It was also during this time that the many hidden sacred libraries opened and man's mind awakened to a fuller potential.

The pace was very hectic during this cycle because of the over-stagnation of the star races. This was necessary to keep the balance. The 12 previously unknown star races from the Hidden Planets, invisible to our vision, made contact and shared information.

The last cycle, called *Menehusbi-staruva* (the cycle of great light), ended in February 2011 after we broke away from the tube torus we had been living in for eons. This cycle brought the translation of many records and bodies of information on the science of immortality, the science of peace and the nature of the cycles of dreaming. It was an age of knowledge that birthed us into freedom.

And now life is new, no longer trapped in a cage of beliefs...

From the *Lemurian Records of Life and Death*

Note: For further reading on the information that came through during the additional two cycles see *Journey into the Labyrinth, The Lemurian Science of Immortality, Transmissions from the Hidden Planets* and Almine's forthcoming book – *The Lemurian Science of Compassion*.

BOOK III

Living from the Dodecahedral Fields
and Beyond

The Ancient Lemurian Records of Life and Death

There are 20 cycles of life. We are currently in the 19th one. When we learn to live from the dodecahedral fields, we shall be in the 20th cycle. Then all 20 spheres of the Flower of Life will be lit and godhood shall be a way of life.

Almine

Part I

Nana Nech Bavi Ursata
Naught is as it Seems

Look now we implore, beyond the furthest reaches of sight
For one there is who will bring these writings to light
Cycles of life; a tube torus travelling around
Within its structure a great secret can be found

Like a shell it is, made of superficial life
It represents ascended mastery: the third stage of human life
The Thief represents god-consciousness, between contraction
    and expansion it vacillates
The Juggler is egocentricity, on the little self it fixates

Caught in the movement of its linear time,
The tube torus dictates the pace of life
Look beyond it to what is inside,
See what within the tube torus hides

A luminous light, another cosmos inside
Captured within its linear confines
Shiny and bright with luminosity
Yet the Inner Cosmos is not free

It is our home, or was meant to be
It must move to the middle of the triad to be free
The thief and juggler and clown gather around
And in the middle, the shiny one must be found

The Empath, this captured cosmos is named
But look and know the Empath's games
It is permeable and allows others' energy in
And thus the draining of others' resources begins

The center of attention, it likes to be
Thus it grows in luminosity
"I am special, look at me
In the center of all, I may be"

It claims to have a special place:
The position of the Embodiment it takes
A liar and pretender of great acclaim
It uses the position of the Embodiment to give it fame

These lies for eons were told
As the Empath the center of the triad did hold
How then did it end up in the tube torus's cage?
When for eons it had usurped the Embodiment's place?

How did it move from its central point;
Why did it with the tube torus join?
So long had it stolen others' energy to survive
It could not on its own stay alive.

Part II

Karus Haresta Pravechbi Unes
The Root of the Antagonism of the Poles

The Empath, a cosmic luminous sphere
Was the origin of the artificial emotion, fear
It caused protectiveness in the Clown
And anger in the Thief could be found

The Juggler vacillated between joy and pain
As the Empath came and left again
The Empath feared it could not survive
Unless on others' energy it thrived

Thus the Empath games contrived
Conflict to create and others to divide
Thus it managed life to polarize
Which to the Empath, much energy did supply

"Save me, save me!" it did cry
Thus the tube torus did comply
"The others are trying to invade me," it lied
"Within your folding embrace let me hide"

But it stole the energy, once inside
Siphoning it off, like a thief in the night
Until the tube torus almost died
Faster it turned, just to survive

The Empath's brilliant luminosity
Comes from others' stolen energy
Look in your own lives and you shall see
That "helplessness" is the greatest form of tyranny

The three cosmoses that linear change represent
Must surely come to an end
But each time, by the Empath they are remade
To have to survive alone, the Empath is afraid

The Embodiment of the Infinite shall the Empath remake
Instead of the sphere, a flower of life it shall create
Nineteen spheres within the one is its form
Thus the Empath into godhood is reborn

Around the nineteen spheres, a double membrane lies
The inner is masculine, the feminine is outside
The receptive feminine invasion does invite
The masculine separates and divides

The shape is obsolete that is described
The feminine should be within, the masculine outside
The field between the two has been abandoned for long
An artificial membrane that steals memories replaced what there belongs.

The Flower of Life Spheres
Before Restoration

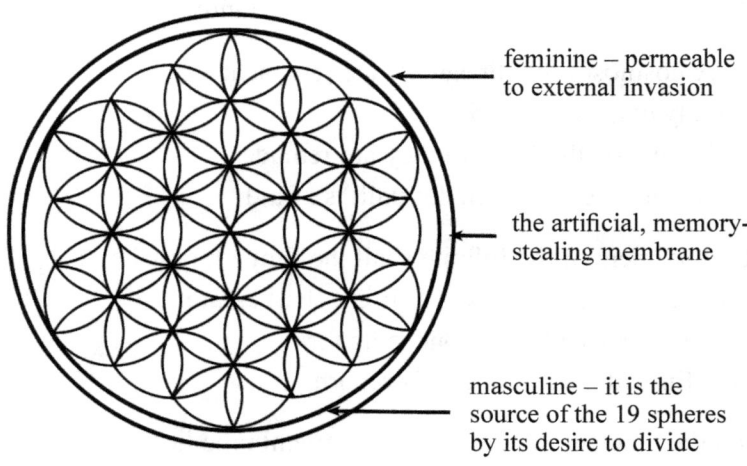

feminine – permeable to external invasion

the artificial, memory-stealing membrane

masculine – it is the source of the 19 spheres by its desire to divide

Figure 29

After Restoration

The separate spheres become a unified field during the first stage of restoration. The second stage of restoration extends the field to include the outer rim.

masculine – repels outer invasions

filled by the *Frequency of Inspiration* through Erotic Interaction

feminine – inclusive rather that divisive

Figure 30

Part III

Naruk Sachve Ereshti
The Song of the Five Elements

Long did it last, the tyranny of the child
Before as a parasite in the tube torus it did hide
How did it hold its unholy rule?
The same way persuasive leaders have controlled you

The element of metal – much over-looked
The song of metal, the controllers took
It holds within it, the tone of majesty
Which can be used to perpetuate tyranny

Both government and religions too
Have used the power of metal to control you
How do they know how it is done?
Long ago with a race called the Annunaki, was it begun

They came from the stars to steal the Earth
To a rule of metals did they give birth
They found that when gold and silver did abound;
When the rulers it did surround

Their power grew and their influence too
Thus the practice grew, gold to accrue
Copper and iron, free choice undermined
And enslaved the children of mankind

When all had gold – the populace too
Freedom of thought and artistry grew
Civilizations rose when this was done
When gold belonged to everyone

The other elements are misunderstood as well
Take time to hear the story they tell
Water, which also within you dwells
Has fluidity, but great power as well

Deep as the ocean that with salt can heal
Unresolved emotions mankind feels
The minerals in your body, with the water combined
Can clear old emotions through intent of mind

Metal when molten; at the moment it liquefies
Releases its power before it solidifies
By being at one with metal's song
Its power to you as well belongs

Fire as passion within us burns
To de-structure old patterns that else would return
Within matter the power of the senses resides
And wind will empty the clatter of mind.

Part IV

Nesetuk Maneshve
The Lost Song

Because the songs of the elements did not fully sing
Consequences to all life this did bring
Each separation of an inner song
To an accompanying illusion does belong

Sexuality became hollow when the illusion of creation began
Nothing new can be created, you must understand
It is self-enjoyment of another as yourself
Procreation is not a justification for a love affaire with self

Work and responsibility, like a necessary evil became
When it instead should be a joyful game
It is a reverent prayer; an act of devotion
A chance for innovation, each task a testimony of self-adoration

Work's pleasure fled when an illusion began
That the little self can achieve, and ambition riddled man

Romance too lost its music when sentiment took its place
The selective valuing of things and events that previously took place
It was meant to be a love-song to life
The love of existence, to elevate humankind

Beauty is not an external standard, it was never meant to be
It has no opposite, when its music is set free
Beauty is a perspective that helps you truly see
The divinity in all life that unfolds eternally

Truth has become archaic – a remnant of the past
Because life changes, yesterday's truth can't last
Truth is the clear participation in unfolding life
The clarity of complete surrender; dissolving inner strife

Relationship was never meant to be based on need
On lust or loneliness, or desperate greed
It is a game of self-inspiration that in others you seek
The praise-worthy in another, is yourself that you see

Freedom is new-found boundlessness that has always been
Even though you thought it lost, when you couldn't see
Love is the resonant response to another's harmony;
That which resonates with our own frequencies

Impeccability is not a set of rules
But knowing there's no choice for the little you
The greater self dictates all you do
Inspirations come from truly seeing another and allowing them to inspire you.

Part V

Kashu Anach Savati
The Unlived Possibilities

The Flower of Life spheres of lower consciousness
Of seven emphasized spheres consist
The higher consciousness that among them exists
An additional eight spheres to Earth life contributes

On Earth five spheres thus have been unlived
Unable the fullness of their blessings to give
Illusions have kept them from being expressed
Banish illusion; no more shall they be suppressed

The intelligent cooperation of opposite poles
Means that our choices must enhance both roles
That full authentic expression can take place
That all value judgments be erased

Let greatness inspire its opposite pole
No longer shall one be robbed, that the other be whole
Limited resources caused this to be
An illusion it is that resources we need

The illusion of division causes it to seem
That there a limited supply of resources have been
Remove this illusion and antagonism will cease
Between the poles, that greatness can be

Know now the song of the elements within your cells
And hear their message very well:
Like the wind that blows and the water that flows
No purpose to life you need to know

It is a privilege to dance upon life's stage
You are not needed, yet invited to participate
If you think you are needed, tension will arise
And neediness to support the agenda inside

Poles have to speak a language that by both can be translated
That dynamic balance can be instated
Erotic responsiveness between the poles
Makes a love affair of life, with each playing a role

The fifth and last sphere that must be lit
Has a great insight associated with it
Why is deceit so easy to perpetrate?
Why do those of integrity not see before it's too late?

Contracted vision is to blame
That we cannot see through deceitful games
The purpose of life is self-appreciation
Accomplished through the perspective of self-exploration

In order to discover what we already know,
We block out some things, others to show
We highlight parts, new perspective to gain
Thus the adventure of rediscovery always remains.

Part VI

Spehesbave Nenuk Harasat
The Power of Language

Words each have a resonant song
Depending on what letters to them belong
The alphabet of humanity of twenty six letters comprised
Representing the god and goddess archetypes

The alphabet of the Original Ones, of higher consciousness
Of only twenty-four letters consists
They only have twelve each of god and goddess archetypes
The thirteenth pair were not needed in their lives

Polluted they have been, the divine archetypes
Thus so has the letters we speak or write
The resurrection of the archetypes into their true meaning,
Of the repair of the alphabet, is the beginning

When spoken, the combined alchemical frequencies, form high alchemy[62]

---

62 High alchemy has the alchemist as part of the equation.

Alchemical Equation

Man's original alphabet:

>   The dissolving of all sub-creations

>   +

The Original One's Language:

>   Humble surrender to Indivisible Source

>   =

Jointly they form:

>   Self-sovereignty through full Resonance

Almine's note: The letters R and W are not in the language of the Original Ones. The original language of man is scattered among the nations, even though in some cases the meaning may have been lost or the words inverted (la = all).

Book III – Living from the Dodecahedral Fields and Beyond

Languages of the
Embodiment of the Infinite

Introduction to the Languages of the Infinite

Whatever is spoken in Mother's languages becomes reality. Having this power, Her languages and their use constitute a most holy body of white and beneficial magic.

The purity of the languages makes them incapable of being misused. The use of these languages brings light and restores perfection. They are without doubt the most holy symbols on earth.

The languages have provided a guidance system for the cosmos. The choice of a specific language of Mother used during a given cycle of Creation provided the exact frequencies and amount of light needed at the time.

The fourth language of the Mother has never been spoken in our vast strand of cosmic clusters. It could only be accessed when we entered a parallel strand or reality where we had never been previously, as will be described later in this section.

The Power Source Wheel

This sacred diagram of sigils calls upon the Mother's power. The three languages are ones Mother has used during different creational cycles. It is also the Power Source Wheel of Belvaspata.

Figure 31

The Second Language of the Holy Mother
Used during the Cosmic Ascension

Excerpted from *The Ring of Truth*

Pronunciation of Mother's Language

The pronunciation is very much like German, other than that the 'v' (as in very) and 'w' (as in white) are pronounced as in English.

The syllables are pronounced individually when placed next to each other. There are no contracted sounds like 'au' (as in trauma). It would be necessary to say the 'a' and 'u' separately. The only exception to this rule is a double 'aa' at the end of a word. This indicates the 'a' sound (as in spa).

The 'ch' spelling at the beginning of a word is the only time it is pronounced as in 'church'. Everywhere else it is pronounced as in the German 'kirche' or somewhat like the Spanish x as in Mexico.

- 'u' is pronounced as in 'prudence'
- 'a' is pronounced as in 'garden'
- 'e' is as in 'pet'
- 'i' is pronounced as in 'pink'
- 'o' is pronounced in the way someone with an English accent would say 'of' or 'cross'
- 'g' is always a hard 'g' like 'great'
- 'c' is always hard as in 'call'
- 'q' has a 'qw' sound as in 'queen'
- 'r' is slightly rolled 'rr'
- 'y' is pronounced as in 'Yvette', with an 'ee' sound

There are many words for 'I' or 'is' because of frequency changes. "I am happy" has a much higher frequency than "I am tired", and "I" or "am" would therefore be different in each of these sentences.

Also, when the concept is large, several words are needed. 'Beautiful' will have different words depending on what is described, but in each case the term will have several words since it is a complex concept.

There are no words for 'sad', 'pain', 'angry', 'protective' or 'fear', since those are illusory concepts in this creation of life. There are also no negative words.

'I' and 'we' would be the same word as this is a group consciousness language. Similarly, 'he' and 'they' would use the same word.

Sentences and Phrases:

1. *Aushbava heresh sishisim*
   Come here.

2. *Va-aal vi-ish paru-es*
   Do it again.

3. *Kre-eshna sa-ul varavaa*
   It is beautiful everywhere.

4. *Pranuvaa sanuvesh vilsh-savu bravispa*
   We are with you when you think of us.

5. *Aasushava pre-unan aruva bareesh*
   We come to open the gate.
   Note: 'Come' in this sense is not the same word used for 'come here'.

6. *Oonee varunish heshpiu tra barin*
   Everyone is dancing with joy.

7. *Belesh bri anur bra vershpi iulan*
   Take away the frown from your face.

8. *Nen hursh avervi tranuk averva?*
   When comes the moment of laughing?

   Note: There is no word for time.

9. *Nun brash barnut pareshvi*
   Please take us with you.

10. *Vursh venestu parneshtu*
    Magic is in the moment.

11. *Iuvishpa niutrim sarem*
    Great things await.

12. *Ruftravasbi iulem*
    Let the fun begin.

13. *Verluash verurlabaa mi urla set viunish*
    Be prepared for the fulfillment of your dreams.

14. *Be-ulahesh parve mi-ur ville starva*
    Speak to us through these sacred words.

15. *Truaveshviesh aluvispaha maurnanuhe*
    Welcome to the fullness of our being.

16. *Telech nusva rura vesbi*
    Through love are we connected.

17. *Erluech spauhura vavish menuba*
    Find the new song that you sing.

18. *Me-uhu vaubaresh ka-ur-tum*
    Our new dance is a joyous one.

19. *Pelech parve uru-uhush vaspa pe-uravesh ple-ura*
    Together let us create wondrous moments.

20. *Vala veshpa uvi kle-u vishpi ula usbeuf pra-uva*
    You are invited into the loving embrace of our arms.

21. *Perenuesh krava susibreve truach*
    In great mercy you are renewed.

22. *Pleshpaa vu skaura versebia nunuhesh*
    Allow your shoulders to feel lightness.

23. *Verunachva ulusetvaabi manuresh*
    All are in this moment redeemed.

24. *Keleustraha virsabaluf bra uvraha*
    You dwell in us and are ours.

25. *Keleshpruanesh te le-usbaru*
    Call and we shall hear.

Alphabet of the Holy Mother

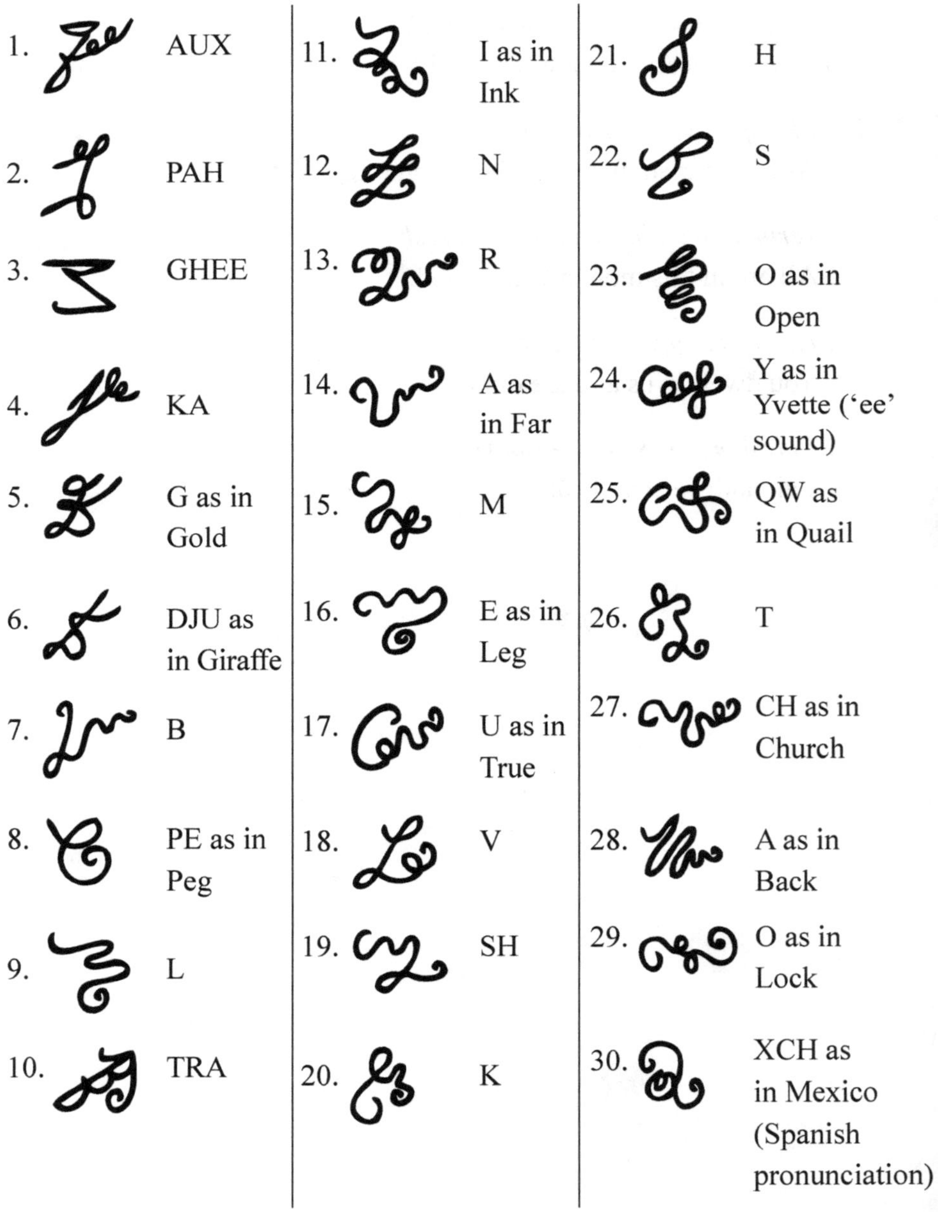

1. AUX
2. PAH
3. GHEE
4. KA
5. G as in Gold
6. DJU as in Giraffe
7. B
8. PE as in Peg
9. L
10. TRA
11. I as in Ink
12. N
13. R
14. A as in Far
15. M
16. E as in Leg
17. U as in True
18. V
19. SH
20. K
21. H
22. S
23. O as in Open
24. Y as in Yvette ('ee' sound)
25. QW as in Quail
26. T
27. CH as in Church
28. A as in Back
29. O as in Lock
30. XCH as in Mexico (Spanish pronunciation)

Figure 32

Alphabet of the Holy Mother
(continued)

Additional Letters of Other Languages Used in the Holy Mother's Language

31.  F
32.  Z as in Azure (soft sound)
33.  RR (rolled r)
34.  P
35.  Y as in Yes
36.  CK (short K sound)
37.  Period (placed at the end of sentence)
38.  Question mark (placed at the beginning of sentence)

1.  D
2.  PF
3.  KL
4.  W
5.  SHP
6.  KRR
7.  HF
8.  PL
9.  TL

Figure 33

The Language of the Holy Mother

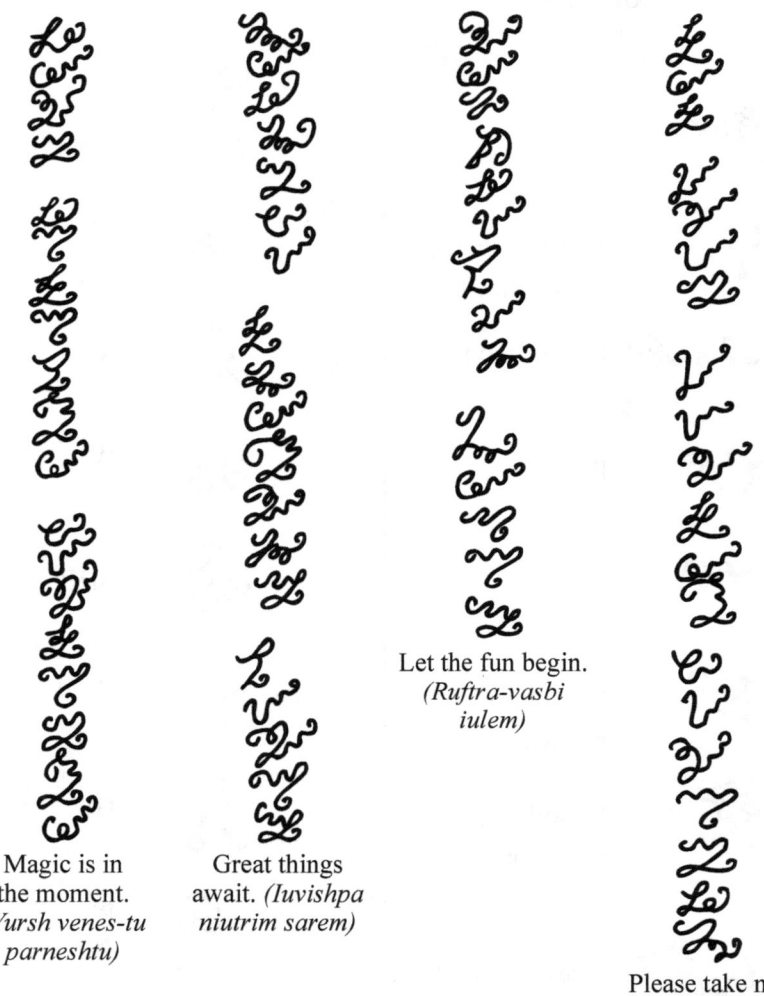

Magic is in the moment. *(Vursh venes-tu parneshtu)*

Great things await. *(Iuvishpa niutrim sarem)*

Let the fun begin. *(Ruftra-vasbi iulem)*

Please take me with you. *(Nun brash barnut pareshvi)*

Figure 34

The Body of Magical Incantations From the Mother of All Creations
(Given in Ireland)

I surrender to the flow of life
Bra u va stichbi satshu u va vesbi kla u taa
Pre u nisbi sta-u-vet blesh pra u vra nesbi sti-u-vaa

I am without self-centeredness and ego
Bra u va beshba kla u vestra baa staurat
Kru na ve vaa stiurech vabaa bla-uvatat
Kla u nish pre ru rish uva-trauvat

I replace impatience with tolerance
Barsh ba na u va ves plavi
Skaura tra nesh va urespi
Gelshtri satvu menuret
Pil blechvi sta-a-rok preuvet

I live a meaningful life through the heart
Tra u bishvaa kre u nit stabaa
Bla u satvi tra-u-bech bilsh vil ste vaa
Gru nit vich versh uris brik belechvi starvaa.

I am self-referring for approval
Blaa blas vaa urvechspi balanech staurek steuravet
Vilsh spaa hirsh vaa achvaa stuaret
Mil skla ra vechspi usvaa kletsut manaret

I realize my infinite potential
Ske la hishvi klabaresh vi klavanet
Spe u va vechspi bilsh paa varnabet
U-a-lechbi stel hu birsh plavet

My being is my sustenance
Paleshu stabalut hechspa urarespi klauvet
Min hursh trauch belchspa vires trua mish baret

I trust in my growing perception and wisdom
Bra bas va vik nichtu birs has vatraa
Pli echvi satru has vra vi us va baa

I dedicate my life to the service of the Mother
Ba ruspa hiresh uchvaa arestaa
Tri esh vi A-ru-ma stelavi stechvi ustaa

May my work enhance all life
Bresh bras ba taa kri ech vi varustet
Bil eshbi klanuch stelvi birsh bak sta-u-vet

My path with heart brings a flow of abundance to me
Birs bra stuvechvi sta u blit bra u-sta-na vik
Sitba eleskru avra vich sta u bla vi setvi nin huravit

My home reflects the beauty, love and grace of Mother
Sta bil pre nu vasbi ura-ech vaa kle vu vraa
Bil-esh sta vi u val vu klavunesh pri I Ma-urva servutaa

I reflect Mother by living my highest truth
Pelesh virstaa ursvaa vechspi uvaklut
Pri satvu klish Vraa-Maa urstanivu barut

I express the love I feel for myself
Birnik blesvaa tra-ug nesvi hareshveg tra-ubit
Erch na klatvu ursvaa staug nar-na-vit

I pull in a compatible romantic partner
Barareshvi traunag eles vich va speleru
Birch nasvi kel u trasvaa birs prak par-navu
Vi veshvi skelug bra ura rak spa ves va-vu

I am free to express Mother's will through my life without restrictions
Balish presvaa kriutug nesvaa iuret
Pliu setvi kleshbaa Ma-us-vaa kliuvet
Ere vechvi sta-u bilevesbi arch ba vet

I have love and compassion for all beings
Traus biles va kresbi sta-u-vech vaa vi
Kles tru ba arch nun belsh bre sit vu as-vaar-vi

I live in eternal time
Barus virna vil pla hes vaa uravach
Birtl birna bil us varas vilsh per vach

All illusion of disease is removed from every child
Brachvaa belishvi nanhur varsh
Pilechvaa strachvaa uresvi sars
Kilespaa nus avrevaa hus
Brachnut selvi stravavek blut

I live in peace and grace
Balech truas stelvi klasvarut
Selbi kleshvaa urvech stavablut

I release all fears
Tre pasvaa kelesvi hech brach bra nas par vi
Granug belech urva birvespi

I live with an open heart, trusting in the perfection of life
Ba u va spiva alech nusva heresvi
Sti ba us plevataa nuchvi stararok blesbi
Kre u basva sistu-esvi bela bechsbi

I replace low self-esteem with visions of my infinite worth
Trach ba ste-u-bi kla-u-vechspi aruret
Mish trechva selvuvaa tra-ba-hesvi-klavunet
Bish nachvaa urech spelvabi sklavuvet

I speak fluently
Ste-u-va-vet plesh nit eresvaa
Kli-u ves vaa urva hesva uspataa

I sing beautifully
Ste-u-pla us va vet nu stavahu sparut
Nun klesh pri-u-nit selvavu hurarut

I create success confidently
Ba uch stavet venush plashet
Ustaa parvi u-berech klanavi
Hersvaa kliu helesbi kresbaa steluch vilesvi

I remove the illusion of disease from all
Parsk klaa bra us vaa virich nis veresvaa
Stalich binahur stel u virskla viresvaa

I teach a path of light
Tra bish kle u varski birsvaa nihurset
Pre-usvaa keluvrig nan hur avraset

My body beautifully reflects perfection
Klaus pirs kla vi argva subatvi hesh
Trech naharvur selbavi klavatur esh
Birsk kla vis peleshvur nanabur barvesh

I integrate the material and spiritual realities
Bra skruvanak eleshvi krachvabu stauret
Bel esva bri stararut mish presvi klauret

I am able to clearly hear and see the spiritual realms
Kritnut peles vusba vis tele huspa kle-rek nus
Trech urvi stararut pelechvi vara vus

I speak my wisdom and truth freely
Ba res pi elech spa uvra vish prech parvi
Nun hesvi klaug spa u rech ru trech varv

My life is filled with joy, courage and self-confidence
Tra bich vashvi klesvaa elech nustaver pri parvat
Bru sta vra vi kelush birk nat vilech stra bar vu vas

I am free to create my life
Talech vis vatra bi elech nur stavet
Ulech bar usva stela birsk

My needs are met effortlessly
Spalech breshva kluaneg
Birspa echva strava hut
Veleshpi skrachva nusvaveg
Rut stanu eles klatvuvet

My life is balanced in all ways
Tra va bisva kliunesva kriuta
Bir ha va kresbi struba vesbi varuta

Each moment I am becoming a greater expression of the perfection of my being

Barich netva arva hursh
Stelaa birsvaa arech nus
Prispraa hesvaa urba setvi baa
Kliu setvaa triu naa
Birtlvit stachvi klesh us bastaa
Hurva nit pre uva silbi hesva-taa

The Third Language of the Mother[63]
Used before the Fall of Creation and restored to Earth March 23, 2007

Introduction

The language illustrated in the following information, given in April 2007 by the Mother, is a language that returned to Earth after the removal of illusion as a reality. All unknown portions of Her Being (illusion) had been solved in August 2006, but the dark gods and goddesses representing illusion lingered until April 2007. When the discordance of their presence in the cosmos was removed, this language in its purity was restored as a gift of enlightenment within the cosmos.

Ex[64] vi ya sha ush hu vi a su bish va ya
Me u vas ba ux sa ush va us vasta
Yo sa vi pa ux mi hesh pa u neesh
Vel es nus va uf vel e nus ta veesh

You may well wonder where the Fall began
It was long before the descent of man
That the hunger for power created a plan
To subdue the Mother and gain the upper hand

Va ul va vix u va cha u ve
Mi ka ul sa u ba vetch sta u ne
Pelesh pfa uf va bash kya va vish
Mex sta ko e yo ash va nu sa ba va nish

---

63 See earlier section Book II, *Eight Cycles Ago*.
64 Pronounced like 'Mexico' in Spanish.

It is with joy that a king of truth[65] is found
When in gods' hearts only greed abounds
But great is the grief to Mother's heart
As She discovers his heart is dark

Ka ush mish kanash ula ve kya u ya
Mish va stua vi a ax nush vya u
Os kyo ush na shu sha shaan
Viya yo sta u nesh vi ash vastaa

Of the gods of the Earth revered by man
But few could the test of power withstand
Most were swept away this day[66]
Condemned by their hearts, they could not stay

Alsh vaa sta u bash va e yo
Pa lux bi ya ka vish vel stash u va so
Mix kya no se va klua uush ma u naa
Pfe elex cha vaa unes staa

Among men, gods and goddesses too
Through ascension raised, to godhood new
Fell from their former high estate
Few there were that kept the faith

Ush kush vas ba vi elsh klaa u na vix
Sta u va yo kna u vish ma na nix
Kelesh u staa pelsh nu kya va u nu
Usha sha naa balex nus us staa vu

---

65 He was an imposter.
66 April 2, 2007

This is the day the nine great lords
Who once governed light from Amenti's Halls[67]
Fell from power and ceased to be
Because of their treachery, lust and greed

Ba aalsh nu vie klas va sut va klex va taa
Mix kyaa vaa u ox tchaa nana vyaa
Shpa su shu ash va us kye nu na te
Mitchaa ex kye belesh baa kla va ye

A day of purging of once trusted ones
Preparing for a time of purity to come
When love shall flow forth to everyone
The reign of the Goddess has begun

Received from the Mother, April 3, 2007

Viya se pa ush ta a va vexh spa u
Va vesh ta ubaxh ya sta va
Mixh kiyè su uva vish tya ba u va veesh cha unaxh
Pè i ye keu cha u viva uva bya

The way of ascension Earth was to take
By dark ones blocked, was difficult to make
Often she tried, as often she failed
On that route too many entrapments lay

Kye usta u elesh vyi ax vaunesh
Ba u vyi esva ucha vaa
Pyè kya uva viesh sta uva bya ka
U vyesbi uva vish byex kava

---

67 For more information on the Halls of Amenti, see *Secrets of the Hidden Realms*.

Thus Mother stepped in to find a way
That she no longer in density stayed
Wayshower to all she had become
For the cosmos she was the archetypal one

Ka vash kya va uva vesh biyè
Cha u ni va viesh ba u neesh
Kyes pa kyesh cha va ustè
Velesh biyexh usta pa u vanyex

Over the edge of space she did ascend
Pulling the cosmos over the bend
Leaving the dark gods to rethink their plans
To try and stop her if they can

Bau kya u spa ba vi klaesh usba
Klau vex bi sta u kla vaa us
Tya u pfyos ba usta biex klash
U na viesh kla u hesh bi esh

But many of us had lost pieces of ourselves,
Dragons and fairies, giants and elves
All were waiting for us on the route
That was abandoned by us—the one we ascended without

Vyioch kelesh ta u va ni-ex
Skla us ta u viyesh sta u na
Knu us sta u kyès ba kli ex
Kla ush cha-usta pli ex na
Us stex kla u kyes ba ux
Cha na nex ki-u belesh bla-a

But that was not all we left behind
Forgotten kingdoms, three of that kind
Each secrets and information held
Each had magic and mystical spells
Thus were those realms called this day[68]
All that was pure could join us to stay

Balu viyex sta u vish kla-u vaa
Kya biyex bi u velesh vi klikla ustaa

When darkness was banished great was the cost
But the new life now would make up for the loss[69]

Almine's Note: The First Language is that of the Embodiment of the Infinite, the Second Language was spoken by Humanity as their original tongue. The Third Language (having only 24 letters), was spoken by the Original Ones. The three represent love, praise and gratitude.

---

68 April 14, 2007
69 There had been a loss of diversity and portions of kingdoms when illusion dissolved. However the diverse life forms on the ascension route we did not take were called into our cosmos and made up for the loss.

The Holy Frequencies

Praise

Love

Gratitude

Figure 35

Part VI

Spehesbave Nenuk Harasat
The Power of Language
(continued)

The combination of archetypes through the power of speech
Became distorted when pure expression ceased
The absence of frequencies created a need
For that which is artificial, the gap to heal

Thus the artificial emotions arose
And the heart of all beings began to close
Look now for the root of why pure expression declined
Guilt is the culprit, you will find

Authentic expression, in the absence of mind
Is the source of power that creates life more refined
But when guilt is present, you will find
An unwillingness to be powerful amongst humankind
Thus full expression is left behind.

Part VII

Parsu Nenechva Harstusat
The Origins of Guilt

The development of the illusion that external power sources exist
Came from our denying the power that is
It is from this, polarity arose
With guilt and fear of power, the doors of supply closed

Eliminate now the causes of guilt that arise
For it causes the war of the poles within life
Thus further guilt, that others wane while we thrive
Compounds the guilt, that power binds

Examine the causes of guilt you can find:
When others perished, you survived
When others did not have the resources to live, you thrived
The Original Ones grew at the expense of humankind

But this is not so – there is an immediate loss for the gain
This is instantly passed to the opposite pole again
With this knowledge, nothing can be taken
Guilt comes from perception that is mistaken

The many as the one creates the journey of life
But it has been fraught with pain and strife
Guilt arises when it seems we create imperfectly
This seems so because there are parts we do not see

The journey as an adventure, was meant to be
To this end, what is known must become a new discovery
There are parts we do not see deliberately
Through this, the perfection also we do not see

Guilt over choices we made that caused others pain;
Over chances lost that may not come again,
Need to be looked at in another light,
We are guided by the blind spots in our sight

The Dreamer dreams the dream – we cannot make a mistake
We are just permitted to participate
Yet, if we are bound by linear time,
Know that every decision of the moment changes past times

The flaws of the past, no longer are so
They are sublimated, by what in the moment we know
Further guilt from others' expectations ensue
When what they expect, is not what we do

It is a service of the highest kind
When we break the boundaries of others' paradigms
What they feel, is self-inflicted pain
It is their own expectations that are to blame

We feel guilt at losing our mastery
At not being able to live miraculously
But our power by guilt has been suppressed
Only when we know: No power source is needed – can mastery be expressed.

Part VIII

Kalesh Archba Rerukva-ba
Understanding What Opposites Are

When light loses its song; when frequency flees
Or light is absent from a specific frequency
It is like a wound that opens in indivisibility
Scar tissue rushes to fill the cavity

The scar tissue is an artificial overlay
A compensatory reality this creates
It tries to sing the song that is lost
But the distortion of reality, is the cost

The sub-personalities artificially formed
From the missing songs were they born
The songs of abundant life, like notes unplayed
Twenty there are that unexpressed stayed

The absence of the song of the Flower of Life formed
Its divisions and separations were born
The archetypes and sub-personalities came to be
To hold the space that forms from duality

Twenty qualities shall stimulate life once more
When light and frequency shall be one as before
Cease to oppose illusions you find
They are but shadows of songs left behind

Hear now and we'll give you the songs that we know
They are tones through which Infinite life flows
The first quality, a tone that you can find
Is to see with the eyes of a newborn child

All moments are greeted with equal surprise
As though each moment is the first one of life
The tone of new beginnings is the first
The tone of deep contentment follows this

Like the warmth of a fire that spreads through your being
Contentment comes when all striving ceases
Rest in the cradle of ages gone by
In perfect surrender, in timelessness lie

Free from the tension of linear time,
Content just to be in enjoyment of life
The third tone of existence is called the "allness of me"
Knowing yourself to be the only being

No portals exist, no sought after power source
No tyrannies or external force
Nothing is needed for you to exist
Great bliss shall come with knowing this

The tone of allness, completeness brings
A new song throughout your being will sing.

Part IX

Arech Pa Haretu Ninasvi
Allowing Life to Sing

Self-honoring is misunderstood as self-aggrandizement
Arrogance that sees the little self as more important
But the honoring of self is an act of devotion
When it is seen that we are not just the current, but the ocean

The divinity of self, needs to be revered
Greatness brings apprehension – loss of humility is feared
Humility and arrogance are shadows that form
When the concept of the many is born

See now the wonder of each little hair
Of the tireless dance of lungs and the air
Know your own beauty by what around you lies
Your muscles like the hills, your temple's pillars, your thighs

Endless is the song you sing with your cells
It is the fifth tone of which we tell
It comes from living in timelessness;
In finding no boundaries, but being in limitlessness

Sing now the song of infinity
In stillness contemplate an existence of eternity
Feel the ages stop flowing through your veins
Let all separation become whole again

Self-wonderment is the sixth tone of exuberant life to know well
How great the power of a single cell
The cosmos around you just a reflection is
Of all that in a single cell exists

Within a cell, all is known
The body around the original cell grows
From belief systems the organs form
By discarding them, the body as a field is born

Know now the wonder of the oneness of self
The seventh tone of which we tell
All is effected by a life lived well
All is a reflection of the single cell

Oneness knows no directions without or within
Oneness knows nothing ends or begins
There is no portal to another place
No divisions or membranes that create space

A life of clear spontaneity is number eight
No patterns exist that the future dictates
Each is a source that generates
Spontaneous existence that the Infinite creates

Omni-dimensionality is number nine
The separations of dimensions are born of mind
The unseen realms, all dimensions as well
Are refined aspects of a single cell

No need to reach and without to strive
When all within you is alive.

The Tuft of Flowers

by Robert Frost

I went to turn the grass once after one
Who mowed it in the dew before the sun.

The dew was gone that made his blade so keen
Before I came to view the leveled scene.

I looked for him behind an isle of trees;
I listened for his whetstone on the breeze.

But he had gone his way, the grass all mown,
And I must be, as he had been – alone,

'As all must be,' I said within my heart,
'Whether they work together or apart.'

But as I said it, swift there passed me by
On noiseless wing a 'wildered butterfly,

Seeking with memories grown dim o'er night
Some resting flower of yesterday's delight.

And once I marked his flight go round and round,
As where some flower lay withering on the ground.

And then he flew as far as eye could see,
And then on tremulous wing came back to me.

I thought of questions that have no reply,
And would have turned to toss the grass to dry;

But he turned first, and led my eye to look
At a tall tuft of flowers beside a brook,

Book III – Living from the Dodecahedral Fields and Beyond

A leaping tongue of bloom the scythe had spared
   Beside a reedy brook the scythe had bared.

I left my place to know them by their name,
   Finding them butterfly weed when I came.

The mower in the dew had loved them thus,
   By leaving them to flourish, not for us,

Nor yet to draw one thought of ours to him.
   But from sheer morning gladness at the brim.

The butterfly and I had lit upon,
   Nevertheless, a message from the dawn,

That made me hear the wakening birds around,
And hear his long scythe whispering to the ground,

And feel a spirit kindred to my own;
   So that henceforth I worked no more alone;

But glad with him, I worked as with his aid,
   And weary, sought at noon with him the shade;

And dreaming, as it were, held brotherly speech
With one whose thought I had not hoped to reach.

'Men work together,' I told him from the heart,
   'Whether they work together or apart.'

Part X

Nechbar Misitrechve
Seeing the Unseen

Through lack of use the senses became
That which access to life dictates
Enforcing parts that density creates
The ability to experience the unseen you must reinstate

First the tenth tone you must know
Omni-sensory perception is the tone
Colors must be heard, music seen
Through regular practice this shall be

Then comes the eleventh tone that activates too
When regularly the practice of the tenth you do
The tone of refined perception it is called
A great gift it is, available to all

Only through using all senses at once
Does access to the refined realms come
Feel behind appearances, close your eyes
Practice to know what beyond the obvious lies

The twelfth tone brings living from depth
While the eleventh stimulates a life of width
The ability to experience the depth of life
Comes from living outside of time

Standing in the silent eye of the storm
The silent depths of awareness is born

Slow life down and you will find
The exquisite perfection that within the moment lies
Taste the moments like a delicious delicacy
And the moment will stretch into eternity

The thirteenth tone holds the poetry of life
That which elevates it beyond survival and strife
That which lives with elegance in life's unfolding pace
Which gets off the treadmill of the mindless race

Consider how to make each act inspire,
Lifting the consciousness of yourself and others higher

The fifteenth tone is surrendered pacelessness
Pace is the desire to control through resistance,
Pace is created through contriving difficulties,
By valuing stability over volatilities

Fear of not having what the moment demands,
If it unfolds too fast, we cannot in balance stand
Creates the desire friction to produce,
To slow things down, or mind may be confused

The desire of mind to understand and know
Must be relinquished for the fifteenth tone
Exponential existence beyond linear geometry
Is the way that miracles come to be.

Part XI

Bri-u-esh Aranach Uvesbi
Expectations of Glad Adventure

From imagined dreams, false belief systems came
The sixteenth tone knows life is a game
Carefree adventure is the tone's name
The adventure of moments that are never the same

Surprises challenge our responses to life
Our attitudes make them a pleasant or unpleasant surprise
Prepare to be amazed – life is a treasure trove
Know it to be safe and explore it through this tone

Peace, the seventeenth tone, cannot be at adventure's expense
It is not the familiar, nor static, as assumed by man
Peace is the underlying stillness of life
Even as the adventure on the surface takes flight

The depth of the moment is where peace is found
Knowing the benevolence of life, is where peace abounds

No defensiveness needed in trusting surrender
With an eternal perspective that sees forever
The eighteenth tone releases all anchors that bind
Reference points are fabricated by mind

Reference points, subjection to their tyranny require
They hold you back more, the higher you aspire
The eighteenth tone unencumbered, like a feather on the wind
Is called unselfconscious flow, like an improvised song you sing

The nineteenth tone is transparent clarity
Crystal clear truth in expression, will change humanity
That all may clearly stand revealed
That we may speak truly what we feel

This can only be when we do not need,
The approval of others for our acts and deeds
Living life from tones of clarity
We do not need endorsements from humanity

Know the origins for all you do
In stillness hear the next step for you
The twentieth tone is all-encompassing inclusiveness
The melting of old programs of lower consciousness

All-inclusiveness is divine compassion's frequency
It shelters old programs' tyranny
It transcends genetic limitation effortlessly
The form changes from solid to fluid

All-embracing compassion acknowledges the validity
Of all that exists, whether or not we can see
When it floods the cells of the body,
It removes all cells' rigidity

The Flower of Life sphere no longer can have parts that are separate
The frequency of divine compassion, this eliminates
Like a blended field every cell becomes
In the body it begins, that the many become one

Divine compassion does not come just from the heart
Such divine love, every cell imparts
It is beyond Earthly love, a feeling most refined
It comes from full surrender, in the silencing of mind.

Part XII

Persklahit Nenechvi Aruvas
The Evolutionary Leap

So it is time, balance to bring
To raise the evolution of humanity
That the lower consciousness of those upon Earth
May into higher levels be birthed

The secret lies with the additional pair;
The thirteenth god and goddess that for man is there
They stand in the middle where the Infinite should be
Blocking access to man's divinity

Yet man has only seven directions in his life
Creating imbalance that causes movement, which is linear time
But man has not always thus been deprived
The imbalance from fear of power was derived

The imbalance has caused the masculine to be over-emphasized
Humanity has lived primarily from mind
A sub-personality from its feminine axis was captured
By the spider goddess, and the psyche of man was fractured

Let the sub-personalities of man be the same
As those of higher consciousness – let there be eight
Let balance come through restoration
That man too can rise with higher evolution

Why did spider-woman arise; how did the thirteenth goddess come to be?
How did the web get thicker until man could no longer see?
From the core of the sub-personalities came life's laws
For the Embodiment of the Infinite was at the core

Formed by the Embodiment's intent, now obsolete,
By old words spoken, laws and decrees,
Old truths and yesterday's wisdoms perceived,
Strand upon strand of binding strands came to be

The shadow formed – the goddess of Arakana was conceived
Thought to be holy, we were deceived
By Arakana ensnared and bound,
Man became more and more imprisoned by light and sound

The impeccable warrior god helped release the snares
But now neither must be there
Let old rules and laws no more be seen
Let existence be pristine and free

The Embodiment unfolds without personality
The sub-personalities cease to be
Divine Compassion shatters the patterns of old
No longer do the words of yesterday patterns hold

The Flower of Life sphere, the template of humanity
Becomes an ever-changing field
No ties that bind from that which is gone
All express fully the unfolding existence of the One.

Part XIII

Nuch-tarava Mishtu Aravas
The Deceit of Reality Unravels

What is reality? Let it be known
Let the deceit of reality fully be shown
To understand the meaning of reality,
First we must understand duality

How can the indivisible be seen as duality?
This results when one sense is given priority
When seeing over hearing is preferred,
The song of life becomes unheard

As communication breaks down between the indivisible poles
It is imagined that they stand separate and alone
The imagined gaps that form for each pole
Fill with the unreal to attempt to make it whole

Thus scar tissue forms, artificial, not based on what is true
The scar tissue, is called "reality" by you
Since the dawn of this imagined rift
Two realities side by side exist

The one reality is based on frequency
Its scar tissue is a light-based physical reality
The other is light-based and because it thinks its frequency is gone,
It makes a frequency-based reality that with it belongs

Scar tissue is rigid and distorted in form
A sub-creation, that from incomplete perception is born,
Nothing can be imperfect within the One
But thus the creation of many sub-created realities was begun

Let the song of life – divine compassion be heard
For it shatters the artificial sub-creations that occurred
Let the Oneness of existence be seen
That its pristine indivisibility be perceived

Let the diversity of Oneness be lived and known
Let illusions be dissolved, let the unfolding perfection be shown
Diversity of Oneness is the combined light and tones
That is the alchemical equation of the twenty Flower of Life's tones

It is the way of living stillness within motion
The fulfillment of humanity's evolution
It is the key to unlocking divinity within
The birth of a higher way of peace, it begins

Where division's illusion ceases to be
There is found the beginning of peace
The connecting to the divine through this key,
Brings to all life self-sovereignty

The living of the twenty tones but provides the key
To unlock the countless tones of Infinity
Refined enjoyment of eternal existence, this does provide
Effortless knowing of ourselves as the One, will unfold before our eyes.

Closing

When frequency and light once more unite,
When divine compassion and the Oneness of life
Inseparable become, expressing as one,
A new era of peace on Earth will have begun

The glory of divinity within all
Will be again as it was before the Fall
Yet rich in self-knowledge and so much more
Not innocently unknowing of its own grandeur, as it was before

Life has evolved in refinement of expression
Not for naught have we lived through cycles of ascension and descension
Life is vivid now, like a multi-hued tapestry
Lived in an eternal moment stretching into infinity

The peace we feel, is the peace that perspective brings
Contentment is valued because we knew suffering
Let awareness of the newness of eternal life
End forever polarity's inner strife.

To the One Life, the glory forever and ever.

Almine

Other Books by Almine

A Life of Miracles

Expanded Third Edition Includes Bonus
Belvaspata Section—Mystical Keys to Ascension

Almine's developing spiritual awareness and abilities from her childhood in South Africa until she emerged as a powerful mystic, to devote her gifts in support of all humanity, is traced. Deeply inspiring and unique in its comparison of man's relationship as the microcosm of the macrocosm. Also available in Spanish.

Published: 2009, 304 pages, soft cover, 6 x 9, ISBN: 978-1-934070-25-3

Journey to the Heart of God

Second Edition

Mystical Keys to Immortal Mastery

Ground-breaking cosmology revealed for the first time, sheds new light on previous bodies of information such as the Torah, the I Ching and the Mayan Zolkien. The explanation of man's relationship as the microcosm as set out in the previous book *A Life of Miracles* is expanded in a way never before addressed by New Age authors, giving new meaning and purpose to human life. Endorsed by an Astrophysicist from Cambridge University and a former NASA scientist, this book is foundational for readers at all levels of spiritual growth.

Published: 2009, 296 pages, soft cover, 6 x 9, ISBN: 978-1-934070-26-0

The Ring of Truth

Third Edition

Sacred Secrets of the Goddess

As man slumbers in awareness, the nature of his reality has altered forever. As one of the most profound mystics of all time, Almine explains this dramatic shift in cosmic laws that is changing life on earth irrevocably. A powerful healing modality is presented to compensate for the changes in laws of energy, healers have traditionally relied upon. The new principles of beneficial white magic and the massive changes in spiritual warriorship are meticulously explained.

Published: 2009, 256 pages, soft cover, 6 x 9, ISBN: 978-1-934070-28-4

Other Books by Almine

Opening the Doors of Heaven
Second Edition
Revelations of the Mysteries of Isis

Through a time-travel tunnel, linking Ireland and Egypt, Isis sent a small group of masters to prepare for the day when her mysteries would once again be released to the world to restore balance and enhance life.

They established the Order of the White Rose to guard the sacred objects and the secrets of Isis. In an unprecedented event heralding the advent of a time of light, these mysteries are released for the first time.

Published: 2009, 312 pages, soft cover, 6 x 9 ISBN: 978-1-934070-31-4

Secrets Of The Hidden Realms
Third Edition
Mystical Keys to the Unseen Worlds

This remarkable book delves into mysteries few mystics have ever revealed. It gives in detail:
- The practical application of the goddess mysteries
- Secrets of the angelic realms
- The maps, alphabets, numerical systems of Lemuria, Atlantis, and the Inner Earth
- The Atlantean calender, accurate within 5 minutes
- The alphabet of the Akashic libraries.

Secrets of the Hidden Realms is a truly amazing bridge across the chasm that has separated humanity for eons from unseen realms.

Published: 2011, 412 pages, soft cover, 6 x 9, ISBN: 978-1-936926-38-1

Aranash Suba Yoga – The Yoga of Enlightenment

Almine's yoga for releasing trauma and strengthening the Eternal Song of the Infinite within. *Aranash Suba Yoga* works at a deep core level to assist with releasing trauma, specifically through the effects that the postures, meditations and stretches have on the psoas muscle. This yoga turns its back on the illusions of the matrices and embraces the contradiction of an existence of no opposites. The overall benefit of *Aranash Suba Yoga* is to release the hold of illusion and strengthen the Eternal Song of the Infinite within.

Published: 2012, 116 pages, soft cover, 6 x 9, ISBN: 978-1-936926-50-3

Other Books by Almine

Belvaspata, Angel Healing, Volume I

The Healing Modality of Miracles Plus: The Healing Methods of Enlightenment and Restoration of Inner Divinity, Angel Healing MP3 included

Whether you are a beginner or an experienced master of the miraculous healing modality of Belvaspata, this comprehensive guide is an information rich handbook that will serve as your most valuable tool – a compendium of information for everything you need to know to establish yourself as a practitioner of this miraculous healing modality of the angels. Also included are *Kaanish, Braamish Ananu* and *Song of the Self Belvaspata*.

Published: 2011, 372 pages, soft cover, 6 x 9, ISBN: 978-1-936926-34-3

Belvaspata, Angel Healing, Volume II

Healing through Oneness Plus:
The Integrated Use of Fragrance Alchemy.

Whether you are a beginner or an experienced master of the miraculous healing modality of Belvaspata, this comprehensive guide is an information rich handbook thatwill serve as your most valuable tool – a compendium of information for everything you need to know to establish yourself as a practitioner of this miraculous healing modality of the angels. Belvaspata Volume II includes "The Integrated Use of Fragrance Alchemy," which delivers the method to obtain wellness of the emotional, mental and physical bodies through the combined use of Belvaspata, the alchemy of fragrance and the Atlantean Healing Sigils.

Published: 2012, 467 pages, soft cover, 6 x 9, ISBN: 978-1-936926-40-4

Handbook for Healers

The Healing Wisdom of the Seer Almine

Handbook for Healers is an invaluable tool for anyone interested in self-healing or the healing of others. It offers both practical and spiritual guidance gleaned from the globally acclaimed Seer Almine's advice to her students during the past decade. It reveals vital information on rejuvenating the body and understanding its communication through the language of pain, and many more empowering insights.

Published: 2013, 620 pages, soft cover, 6 x 9, ISBN: 978-1-936926-44-2

Other Books by Almine

Secrets of Dragon Magic, The Sacred Fires of the Hadji-ka

This extraordinary record of the philosophy and practices of dragon magic is unmatched in its depth of knowledge and powerful delivery. From the *Sacred Records of the Hadji-ka*, kept by the dragons of Avondar, the secrets of Kundalini are revealed, designed to restore the innate, natural magical abilities of man lost by the separation of the spinal column and the pranic tube. The reader is swept along on a profound and mystical journey that pushes perception beyond mortal boundaries. Almine's infallible ability to empower her reading audience is clearly felt throughout the pages of this book.

Published: 2013, 400 pages, soft cover, 6 x 9,
$24.95, ISBN: 978-1-936926-56-5

The Sacred Breaths of Arasatma
Alchemcial Breathing Techniques of the Ancients

The Arasatma Breathing Technique was used by ancient mystics to activate the unused portion of the pranic tube for fuller self-expression and inner peace. A fully cleared and active pranic tube is the gateway to a magical life. Also, these breathing techniques aid in the restoration of the subtle, etheric functions of the body and senses. This allows the practitioner to access other dimensions and prolongs an eternal life of graceful unfolding. This book doesn't only share the first 3 levels of this powerful breathing technique but for the first time also publicly shares 3 follow-up levels to those who wish to continue their journey with this powerful transformative tool.

Published: 2013, 363 pages, soft cover, 6 x 9,
$34.95, ISBN: 978-1-936926-64-0

Music by Almine

Children of the Sun

Music from the Known Planets (Re-mastered and re-titled version of the Interstellar Sound Elixirs) The beautiful interstellar sound elixirs received and sung by Almine.

Price $9.95 MP3 Download
$14.95 CD

Labyrinth of the Moon

Music from the Hidden Planets (Re-titled version of the Sound Elixirs of the Hidden Planets) All the vocals in these elixirs are received and sung in the moment by Almine

Price $9.95 MP3 Download
$14.95 CD

Jubilation – Songs of Praise

Music from around the world to lift the heart and inspire the listener. The extraordinary mystical quality of the music, and the exquisite clarity of Almine's voice, creates the ambient impression of being in the presence of angels.

Price $9.95 MP3 Download
$14.95 CD

Additional Products by Almine

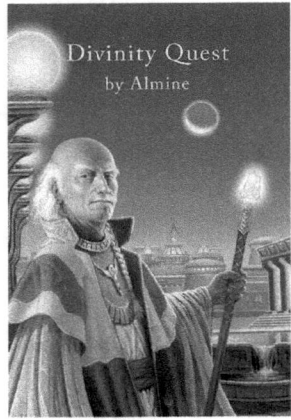

Divinity Quest

Through ages of existence of cycles of life, death and ascension, there are those great lights on Earth who have felt the deep anguish of knowing that the reality of man is not their own; that a higher reality beckons. Almine has laid down a map for the magnificent journey home to the greater reality of godhood.

Divinity Quest is a physical card deck for divination and DNA activation. It's an easy yet profound tool, enabling the remembrance and activation of your divine origin in daily life.

Price $34.95

Visit Almine's website www.spiritualjourneys.com for worldwide retreat locations and dates, online courses, radio shows and more. Order one of Almine's many books, CDs or an instant download. US toll-free phone: 1-877-552-5646

www.ingramcontent.com/pod-product-compliance
Lightning Source LLC
Chambersburg PA
CBHW060352170426
43199CB00013B/1839